PRAISE FOR *CRAZY SCRE*

"Motivating and exuberant, Weiko understands the personal nature of screen-writing . . . provides a roadmap to finding the unique stories each person has to tell and creating screenplays that live and breathe."—**David S. Goyer**, co-writer, *Terminator: Dark Fate, The Dark Knight* trilogy

"Offers a unique culinary glimpse into how films really get made, sold, and released on a global scale from a veteran screenwriter who knows the secret to a successful film career is in the ingredients, not the meal."—**Scott Beck & Bryan Woods**, writers, WGA Award nominees, *A Quiet Place*

"As fast paced and exciting as the commercial blockbusters he references and deconstructs, Weiko's book features a wealth of practical advice for the aspiring and perspiring screenwriter."—**Paul W. S. Anderson**, writer, director, *Resident Evil* franchise, *AVP: Alien vs. Predator, Death Race, Mortal Kombat*

"It's rare to get firsthand knowledge from someone who's been there and done that, but Weiko's *Crazy Screenwriting Secrets* delivers that in a fun and insightful way while sending you on your path to understanding how to get your story to the big screen."—**Andy Horwitz**, producer, *American Hustle, Suicide Squad, Triple Frontier*

"Everyone has secrets; fortunately, Weiko Lin is sharing his. You'd be 'crazy' not to take advantage of Weiko's insights for successful screen-writing."—**Kevin S. Bright**, executive producer, director, *Friends*

"Are you crazy enough to DIG DEEP, work HARD, write and REWRITE until you discover the most inspired version of your screenplay? This book is for you!"—**Felicia D. Henderson**, writer, co-executive producer, Marvel's *The Punisher, Empire, Gossip Girl*

"Comparing screenwriting to preparing a meal—creating recipes, getting ingredients, cooking food—is brilliant. It inspires narrative stories that con-nect us all, regardless of cultural differences. It's logical, fun, easily digested, and delicious."—**Henry Chan**, director, *Scrubs, King of Queens*, Alibaba's *Rich House, Poor House* 王子富愁记, *100 Days* 真爱100天

"Writing is hard. Even this blurb took me days to crank out. So anyone who makes it even the slightest bit easier is a hero. Weiko unlocks the mysteries of the screenwriting craft and entertainment business."—**Courtney Lilly**, writer, executive producer, *Black-ish*

"Weiko's intellect and charisma are on full display . . . crazy insightful."—**Bennett Graebner**, executive producer, *The Bachelor*, *The Bachelorette*

"Weiko's ability to break down scripts and help the writer infuse their soul into their work is why still today his screenwriting class has had the greatest impact on my writing."—**Marisha Mukherjee**, writer, DC's *Titans*, *Quantico*

"A terrific and comprehensive guide to the fundamentals of screenwriting—from finding your inspiration to marketing your work. With his signature enthusiasm and encouragement, Weiko makes the daunting task of writing your first screenplay approachable, and even fun!"—**Meridith Friedman**, writer, *Chicago Med*

"Offers new writers an enthusiastic and positive approach to screenwriting, from brainstorming to business, in an honest, accessible tone. Recommended to anyone starting the intimidating and mysterious process of screenwriting!"—**Stephanie Kornick**, writer, *Transparent*

"My go-to source for motivation, career advice, and perspective on global entertainment."—**Rocco Pucillo**, writer, Netflix's *Voltron: Legendary Defender*

"Explores the absurdity of our story, then helps us fearlessly craft it onto the page."—**Robin Shou**, actor, *Mortal Kombat*, *Beverly Hills Ninja*; writer, director, *Red Trousers*

For more advance praise for *Crazy Screenwriting Secrets*, turn to the back of the book!

Crazy Screenwriting Secrets

HOW TO CAPTURE A GLOBAL AUDIENCE

WEIKO LIN

MICHAEL WIESE PRODUCTIONS

Published by Michael Wiese Productions
12400 Ventura Blvd. #1111
Studio City, CA 91604
(818) 379-8799, (818) 986-3408 (FAX)
mw@mwp.com
www.mwp.com

Cover design by Johnny Ink. www.johnnyink.com
Copyediting by Ross Plotkin
Interior design by William Morosi
Printed by McNaughton & Gunn

Manufactured in the United States of America

Library of Congress Cataloging-in-Publication Data
Names: Lin, Weiko, 1975- author.
Title: Crazy screenwriting secrets : how to capture a global audience / Weiko
   Lin.
Description: Studio City, CA : Michael Wiese Productions, [2019] | Includes
   bibliographical references.
Identifiers: LCCN 2019017701 | ISBN 9781615933013
Subjects: LCSH: Motion picture authorship. | Motion picture
   authorship--China. | Motion picture audiences.
Classification: LCC PN1996 .L55 2019 | DDC 808.2/3--dc23
LC record available at https://lccn.loc.gov/2019017701

First Printing: July 2019
Printed on Recycled Stock

TABLE OF CONTENTS

Dedication vii

Acknowledgments viii

Introduction xi

Part One
GET CRAZY: Writing Tools

CHAPTER 1: FUNNY FARM | Plowing Story Seeds 3

CHAPTER 2: SIGNATURE DISHES | Genres. 11

CHAPTER 3: FIRING UP THE STORY | Protagonist and Antagonist. . . 21

CHAPTER 4: THREE-COURSE MEAL | Movie Structure 33

CHAPTER 5: RECIPES | The Step Outline 40

Part Two
KITCHEN IN THE MADHOUSE:
Screenplay Construction

CHAPTER 6: APPETIZER | Act One—Whet the Palate. 49

CHAPTER 7: MAIN COURSE | Act Two—Savory Climax 55

CHAPTER 8: DESSERT | Act Three—Satisfaction 59

CHAPTER 9: PRESENTATION | Organic Action and Dialogue 65

CHAPTER 10: EMOTIONS | Moving Stories Before Moving Scenes 72

CHAPTER 11: THERAPY | Digesting Notes and Rewriting 75

CHAPTER 12: PROCESS | Always Be Writing 82

Part Three

LEAVING THE ASYLUM: The Writing Profession

CHAPTER 13: WORKFLOW | From Screenplay to Theaters............89

CHAPTER 14: THE TEAM | Hollywood Managers and Agents 95

CHAPTER 15: BREAKING IN | Film Schools and Competitions.......102

CHAPTER 16: COLLABORATION | Working as Partners.............111

CHAPTER 17: PROTECTION | Registration and Copyright...........114

CHAPTER 18: RIGHTS OF ARTISTS | Writers Guild of America......116

Part Four

WHAT A WONDERFUL WORLD:
Universal Movies

CHAPTER 19: GLOBAL FRANCHISE | Connection and Consistency. .121

CHAPTER 20: EXTRACTING CULTURE | Inclusion of Perspectives .123

CHAPTER 21: AWAKENING | Crazy Rich Asians—The New Wave....127

CHAPTER 22: LOST IN TRANSLATION | Creating Stories for
Mainland China...131

CHAPTER 23: CHINESE FLAVOR | Adapting 5,000 Years of Culture
for Global Audiences 141

CHAPTER 24: FUSION | China Coproductions 151

CHAPTER 25: HAVE YOU EATEN? | Chinese Cultural and Social
Etiquettes 156

Part Five

THE CRAZY SECRET

CHAPTER 26: TO LIVE: Fall Into Place 165

Glossary...167

About the Author 169

For my mother, Lisa 張麗春
When you had to go,
you left me the most beautiful gifts to comfort
and guide me the rest of the way

ACKNOWLEDGMENTS

My eternal gratitude goes to legendary UCLA masters Richard Walter, Lew Hunter, Howard Suber, Hal Ackerman, and Dan Pyne; all of whom I've had the privilege of studying with. Their DNA is very much ingrained in this book. They taught me not only the craft of screenwriting, but they instilled ethos in me, inspiring me to become a teacher as part of my writing life. Heartfelt thanks to my managers Robyn Meisinger and Ryan Cunningham who bring out the best wordsmith in me. Do these two know story! Thanks to my agent Max Michael for supporting my crazy ambitious projects for the U.S. *and* China. I want to especially thank Jeremy Zimmer of United Talent Agency for teaching me the business part of show business during grad school that gave me an honest perspective of the industry right from the get-go. Michael Wiese and Ken Lee are true saints for giving breath to this book. Finally, my creative and cultural asylum would not be possible without the Lins, Fans, Mills, Kuos, Smiths, Kuchidas, Chans, Pucillos, Chungs, Bigelows, Satchells, beloved friends, inspiring colleagues, and my passionate students.

INTRODUCTION

"Though this be madness, yet there is method in it."
—**William Shakespeare,** playwright, *King Lear*

As a kid growing up in Taipei, I was obsessed with popcorn Chinese martial arts movies with rehashed premises of a sworn enemy stealing a treasured manual that contained a *secret*, powerful form of martial arts technique. And the hero must find it at all costs to master that technique to defeat the villain. These stories were so delicious! Imagine there was only *one* secret fighting style that holds the key to victory!

Almost every ancient civilization from the Romans, Greeks, to the Chinese had manuals that taught different forms of martial arts just as there are several screenwriting books showing unique approaches. But in the end, the fundamentals are all the same. There is no right or wrong way. The right way is whatever works for you. Just look at today's popular mixed martial arts where fighters extract styles from all disciplines from jiu-jitsu to boxing. They adapt elements that work best for them. The secret essence of this *manual* is simply my distilling of the finest forms and styles of screenwriting from brilliant masters of the craft. Those masters are the teachers, managers, producers, directors, and executives that I've had the incredible fortune to work with.

This manual is your compass. You can get to your destination without it. But it might help avoid detours that can ignite crushing frustrations that sink you into the dreaded purgatory of writer's block . . . and maybe even into surrender.

CRAZY SCREENWRITING SECRETS • LIN

THIS ISN'T ROCKET SCIENCE

When overthinking it, you'll end up spending more time trying to understand the bloated theories instead of getting on with the actual writing. When well-intentioned books and seminars present convoluted graphs and charts in relation to screenwriting, they remind me of that scene in *Dead Poets Society* when the teacher John Keating (Robin Williams) has his students read out loud the introduction chapter on how to appreciate poetry. It theorizes poetry reading with scientific *graphs and charts*! Robin Williams proceeds with instructions to tear up those intro pages! That's exactly what you should do. No, don't rip up your other screenwriting books. There are some excellent ones out there. But if you are spending more time obsessing over the clever science of screenplay than your own writing, take a step back. Better yet, do a complete about face! Screenwriting is tangible to everyone and anyone with an inkling of story in them. The steps are simple. But it takes hard work. A whole lot of blood, sweat, and tears. If you're up for it . . . and I hope you are . . . keep reading!

WHAT DOES CRAZY GOT TO DO WITH IT?

We are all *born crazy*. More specifically, we are born with crazy hearts! *Crazy Heart* is my all-time favorite movie title. The phrase encapsulates the soul of screenwriting. Love can make you so crazy that all logic goes out the door. Love gives you that same euphoric high as watching an imaginative movie or creating that electrifying screenplay.

Let's start with cinematic heroes. They are insane! They act against the norm. They are fearless. Oh, how *we crave that*. They don't play it safe like we do in our daily routines. We watch movies to experience the crazy that we wish we could experience in real life. Taking that risk. Taking that chance.

Who is *crazy enough* to become a male stripper after being laid off in order to keep shared custody of their son like in *The Full*

Monty? Who is *crazy enough* to take on their daughter's human traf-ficking kidnappers in Europe like in *Taken?* Who is *crazy enough* as an eight-year-old boy accidentally left home alone to fight off invad-ing burglars during the Christmas holidays like in *Home Alone?*

Children do whatever their impulses move them to do and say. Adulthood is disciplined with schedules and *sedated* behavior to be "practical." This is what brings law and order to civilization. But a side effect includes repression of our innate craziness.

Whenever you ask a producer or executive what they look for in a writer, they will likely say someone with a "unique voice." But how do you quantify that? Actually, what the heck is a voice? Singing on the page? Voice is something you *feel* when you read it. The voice is your crazy perspective that only you can express. That is what makes your writing and talent shine like a brightly lit star that can be seen billions of light years away.

WHAT'S THE BIG DEAL?

Why give the screenplay so much love and care when it's not even the final product? We watch the actual movie. We don't read unpro-duced screenplays. So what's all the fuss?

The screenplay is the central core that the *potential* of a movie is built on.

It is literally the most important and the only *existing property* before the movie is produced. Thus, the screenplay is referred to as intellectual property (IP). For the sake of clarification, as I refer to "readers" moving forward, I don't mean just the script cover-age writer who has the thankless job of writing the book report on screenplay submissions to agencies, production companies, and stu-dios. I am mainly talking about the readers who are decision makers and collaborators. They are the ones who read the screenplay before production. The script is the talking point of discussion for creative vision and the logistical mounting of the production. Their reactions to the *potential of the movie* will determine the miraculous greenlight to production.

The producers have to believe there is a movie based solely on their *reading* of the screenplay. Then they bring it to the studio executives to *read* the screenplay and make an acquisition decision about the script for development. Even marketing departments will *read* it and project potential sales in America and worldwide. Agents and managers representing directors and movie stars *read* it to see if the project might be a superb fit for their clients. Movie stars and directors *read* it after a thumbs up from their reps. Once the movie is greenlit, hired department heads like the cinematographer, production designer, costume designer, line producer, and casting director all *read* the script as the basis to inspire creativity and logistics in their respective roles making the movie. The screenplay is the central vision for the entire movie production! Thousands of jobs are created around this roughly 105-page document.

This is why studios and financiers spend at times millions of dollars and years of development to ensure that the script is the best it can be before plopping down $100 million to make the movie and at least another $50 million or more to market it. Yikes! So, it better be awesome on the page. This is the reason American movies dominate the global box office. The prioritization of its resources and commitment to script development before a single dollar is spent on production gives Hollywood or America an edge over most other countries that typically dedicate the *least* amount of assets to it. Often times, they simply can't afford to. Development and screenwriting are invisible processes that have been the heart of American film industry's 100-year-plus history. As a result, there are thousands of highly paid and story savvy Hollywood development executives whose primary skillsets are to develop scripts to become worthy of production.

WHO IS THIS GUY?

I can't boast millions of dollars in screenplay sales like some other authors. But I am in the real trenches. I have been paid to write several feature screenplays for both American and Chinese companies. I am a screenwriter with active projects in both the United States and China, the two biggest movie box offices in the world. I've also developed a scripted TV pilot with a U.S. digital studio owned by a major conglomerate that's designed for global intersection. I'm a proud current active member of Writers Guild of America West (WGA, a labor union for professional writers of film, TV, new media) and the Dramatist Guild of America (professional organization for playwrights).

However, my best work yet that has sprouted from this creative life has been in teaching screenplay workshops. Having taught screenwriting at institutions such as UCLA, Northwestern University, Emerson College, and Taipei National University of the Arts, I am so proud of my students who have gone on to write movies for studios such as Universal and Wanda Pictures as well as selling TV pilots to ABC, Comedy Central, and Netflix. Many have blossoming careers writing on shows at all the major networks, including series such as *Transparent, DC's Titans, Man with a Plan, Chicago Med, The Code, DC's Stargirl, Whiskey Cavalier, Major Crimes, Quantico, Murder in the First, Dr. Ken, Heroes Reborn, The Late Show With Stephen Colbert*, and many others. Some have become authors for publishers like Simon & Schuster and Chronicle Books. My Chinese students have garnered Golden Horse Nominations (the Chinese equivalent of the Oscars) for screenwriting. Many other past students are writing with persistence and passion, inching closer to earning their break. But in my mind, it doesn't matter whether they turn professional or not. Writing is a way of life. And for those who *need* to be writers, they certainly are still pouring words onto the pages regardless. My heart is full of pride for them all.

ONE-STOP SHOP

The first half of this book covers the craft: Story Idea, Characters, One-Page Step Outline, and the Screenplay. The second half breaks down the ever-evolving Hollywood system and shares insights on stories that resonate with the world. Specifically, a few chapters cover the explosive Chinese film industry in relation to the U.S. as they intertwine. Having a basic idea of the impact on how movies are produced in a global way, writers can approach storytelling with an inclusive, worldly perspective. First understanding *why* American narratives have global appeal, we will explore *how* Chinese films and non-American movies can craft stories with unique spices of their own culture that can bridge with a worldwide audience. Ultimately, this can inspire you to create and develop movies that not only *move* audiences in your country, but also *connect* globally in the same fashion Hollywood films have done for the last century.

WELCOME TO THE MADHOUSE

Civilization encourages us to play it safe our entire lives. Heck, if we all acted out the craziness like our movie heroes, it would be absolute mayhem! Heroes in movies make crazy decisions and take action from the heart. Something we wouldn't do in reality. Our conditioned minds would stop us. But the heroes help fulfill our inner desires. *And we love them for it.*

Can the *crazy* be taught?

No. But it can be guided and nurtured. Let's *rediscover* that crazy within you.

Part One

GET CRAZY:
Writing Tools

"You're only given a little spark of madness. You mustn't lose it."

—**Robin Williams**, actor, *Good Will Hunting*

Chapter 1

FUNNY FARM
Plowing Story Seeds

*"An artist is a creature driven by
demons . . . He is completely amoral in that
he will rob, borrow, beg, or steal from anybody
and everybody to get the work done."*

—**William Faulkner**, author, *As I Lay Dying*

P assion is a key ingredient to cook up a delicious story. But writing with *compassion* is everything. Passion will champion the characters. Compassion will move the readers. And moving the readers will lead to a "moving film" that they can get behind emotionally. That translates into a script sale! Writing to sell is obviously a sweet motivation. But it cannot be the primary motivation. There are many books that focus on high concepts and how to sell, sell, sell. Tons of them! But pumping out ideas to chase what's hot in the market will turn ice cold by the time you get the movie out. Writing a movie about a school for young wizards like *Harry Potter* or a movie about sexy vampires and hunky werewolves with abs like *Twilight* won't interest the audience today. But you can imagine the sheer number of scripts chasing the trends that flooded the market when those films came out. Being motivated purely by writing what sells will ultimately chip away your soul. I get it. Soul doesn't feed the stomach nor pay the commission to your agents and managers.

Selling scripts and getting hired to write on assignments are how you survive. But the motivation for every project should surge from what story you *need* to tell. A story that will make a difference. What do you want to say that might have an influence? I know what you're thinking. He is treading along the artsy, indie film philosophy. Heck, no! Far from it! You can have something to say in big entertaining movies. Just look at *Get Out*. It's a commentary on systematic racism within the horror narrative that scared its box office to $255 million worldwide on a $4.5 million production budget! And it netted the writer and director Jordan Peele an Oscar for Best Screenplay. Barrages of action and special effects are fantastic visual delights. But don't rely on them to patch up the lack of soul and depth in your stories. The audience will catch on. They are smart as hell. They have a choice in movies. Many choices. Make them want to *choose* yours.

Let's start from scratch.

WRITE WHAT YOU KNOW . . . *NOT*

Unless you've lived a spectacular life like Forrest Gump or you've had specific experiences that are out of the ordinary, don't take "write what you know" *literally*. There are only so many autobiographical stories you can generate for movies. And that won't last a career worth of materials. Absolutely, write something personal in one or two of your screenplays. It can be an emotionally moving sample that no one else can write except for you. It is absolutely imperative that you write what *emotions you know*. You may not have been a billionaire vigilante fighting crimes in Gotham City like *The Dark Knight*, but maybe you have experienced the loss of a parent like young Bruce Wayne did. That universal, human loss emotionally defined Batman and connected us to him.

How did a loss in your life shape your own decisions?

Before getting ahead with all those yucky emotions, how do you tap into story ideas within your fountain of creativity?

REMEMBER THAT CRAZY TIME *WHEN* . . .

Here's a little jump starter. Sit back. Or lie down. Close your eyes. Take a mindful moment. Inhale through your nose. Hold it. Now exhale through your mouth in a steady stream. Repeat twice.

Open your eyes.

Think about a time you have been:

Bad.

Naughty.

Sinful.

Not just thoughts. I mean real action. Something you *did*. Oh, yes. We are going there. That time you did something *crazy!* Maybe you've shared it with friends at a bar after two whiskey sours too many. Or during some late night heart-to-heart dorm hall chat. Maybe you still feel guilty about it to this day. It's buried so deep that you're *afraid* to revisit it. Held it locked in for years. Now it's confession time. No one will ever know except for you. Take five minutes. Write it down. Don't self-censor.

If you're still trying to recall one or have *too many* to choose from, try going back to grade school. Or even from just yesterday! Don't say you've never been *bad*. We have all violated society's gold standard of proper behavior. Stolen for the first time. Betrayed a loved one. Kissed your best friend's lover. Snuck out of the house past curfew. Broken a family heirloom and blamed it on your kid sister.

WHAT IF?

Here's my crazy bad. As a seven-year old in Taipei, it was perfectly normal for first graders to walk home from school by themselves. It was typhoon season. One day, my best friend and I took a detour to trespass a construction site so we could play in the mud! To us, it was a giant playground instead of a danger zone. The skies got dark. We lost track of time playing until typhoon rain started pouring on us. We were late. As we climbed our way out, a man executed a cop right in front of us! We bolted out of there—but he'd already seen our faces! My best friend and I swore to each other to not say a thing to our families. Not to anyone. Next day at school, the killer in a police uniform shows up to our classroom. He pulls us out for "questioning." We didn't resist. Nobody would have believed us. As he shoved us into his car, we knew this was it. We had to escape or we were goners—okay, I will stop there. You probably caught on that I was making it up. *But not all of it.* Everything was true up to the point that we realized we were late to get home. We saw no cops. No murders. But *what if* we had? Yes, it was *crazy* to play on a construction site. But by adding the extraordinary situation of witnessing a cop murder, that's what sets up a potential premise of a movie. In the end, my pal and I got home just fine. My parents weren't even that worried. They just scolded me to not play at construction sites again. Of course we went back the very next day . . .

By combining the *crazy* and the *what if*, you've got the potential premise for a screenplay that not only rings true but also fuels a cinematic narrative.

INFLUENCES

Artists are often scared of stealing at the risk of being unoriginal. We second guess potential ideas if they seem even remotely similar to an existing movie or feel like they've been done before. That may be the case.

But it hasn't been done by you.

Embrace inspiration of other movies and literature in your work. The good ones. If you ask any professional singers and bands, they will cite influences of other artists on their own music. The story is filtered through your *unique voice. Armageddon* and *Deep Impact* have a near identical idea about a group of humans who land on an asteroid/comet to destroy it before colliding with earth. But they have two completely different narrative executions. This is the reason why you cannot copyright an *idea*. You can only copyright the expression of that *story*.

FAMILY

If you are stuck coming up with a story, start with family. Most films are essentially about families. Every human on this planet can relate to it. That's why people love them. I love stories about broken families and their fight to keep it together. *Kramer vs. Kramer. Crash. American Beauty.* All winners of Best Picture Oscars. But it's not limited to birth families. Alternative families like the soldiers in *Saving Private Ryan* and *Platoon* resonate. Just like how the outcast mental patients forming their own special family in *One Flew Over the Cuckoo's Nest* also connects with the audience. Tentpole movies like *Armageddon* have family at their emotional core. Harry Stamper (Bruce Willis) goes on a suicide mission to save the world in order to earn the respect and love of his daughter. Even genre horror movies like *A Quiet Place* and *Poltergeist* are about parents fighting to keep the family *alive*. Crime dramas like *The Godfather* are about men who will protect their families at all costs. In *Rain Man*, two estranged adult brothers come together after the family broke apart during their childhood. Even my crime thriller script *Chalk* that was a finalist in Academy of Motion Pictures Arts and Sciences Nicholl Screenwriting Fellowship was about three estranged adult brothers reuniting with their drug addict mother after she witnessed the murder of a police officer.

PERSISTENCE

If you want to start with a theme, try this one. When considering all the timeless American movies, the majority of them are about persistence. Forrest Gump (Tom Hanks) never gives up on his love for Jenny in *Forrest Gump*. Rocky Balboa (Sylvester Stallone) "goes the distance" in *Rocky*. Chuck Noland (Tom Hanks) fights to survive on a deserted island in order to reunite with his wife in *Cast Away*. In *Shawshank Redemption*, innocent convict Andy Dufresne (Tim Robbins) chips a tunnel through his cell wall with a toothpick-sized rock hammer over the course of nineteen years!

THE LIVING DEAD

My go-to place for character inspiration is the *Los Angeles Times*. More specifically, I scour the obituary section for articles about really fascinating people who had recently passed away. The key word is *people*. Not characters. Their *real* lives were obviously interesting enough to garner a feature editorial. Sometimes kernels of that person's life can *inspire* characters and even stories in your own scripts. Most of the time, there is always a facet of their lives that sticks with me. Any element that catches my emotion or attention, I jot it down. They may come to life later that month. The next year. Or even the next decade.

MARINATE IT

When you have ideas for a screenplay in your head, write them down! No matter how good they are and no matter how spectacular your memory is, you will forget them. I promise. When they're written down, you feel responsible for them. Creativity needs to be marinated. They will always be richer in flavor after they soak in your brain for a while. I keep three mini-notebooks bound with a rubber band with me at all times. One for *character*, one for *story*, and one for *dialogue*. I compile sketches of people, ideas, and dialogue I have resonated with either in real life or from my readings.

Now in the digital age, you can use a smart phone. It's something that's literally tethered to you. You can even record it and type them up later. If you are a tech moron like me, email is a way to go. You can set up a separate, exclusive email where you can send the ideas. This way, they don't get lost and cluttered in your personal inbox. While on set directing his comedy feature *The 40-Year-Old Virgin*, writer and director Judd Apatow emailed himself the initial ideas and story breakdown for *Knocked Up* on his Blackberry. Remember those killer keyboards? I miss them. Be sure to label the subject Character, Story, and Dialogue so it will be easy to search and categorize. That same email can be used to send back-up drafts of your scripts. Do whatever works for you. Just make sure you have a system. Whenever you find something moving or interesting in an article, book, or anecdote from friends, record it in the respective notebook or electronic storage of your choice. Most times, the story isn't really a story. It can be a small slice of life. You had a reaction to it. There must be something there that you can channel emotionally. Sometimes the story becomes a potential screenplay many years after you had written down the genesis of it.

CRAFTING THE LOGLINE

Once you have formulated the movie concept or idea, the next step is to put it in a logline. The English literature major in me would say this is the thesis of the movie. Check out Fandango. Or even Wikipedia for reference. One to two lines are ideal. Pick a movie that's closest in genre or story to what you plan to write. Study how the logline is put together. A logline isn't just for the marketing and promotion of a movie. It's the short hand to articulate what your script is about. It's what producers, directors, actors, agents, and managers use from a script's development all the way to the movie's distribution. Run it by friends. See if it's something they'd pluck down their hard-earned $20 to watch. Think of the logline as the trailer of the script. Use the least amount of words to express the most. The next chapter on genres will have several samples to check out.

WHAT WILL YOU DIE FOR?

You've now got two or several loglines you want to turn into screenplays. So how do you assess which one to dive into *now*? This is usually when your manager and agent can serve as sounding boards. But if you are working without representation, ask yourself this: *What will you die for?* Every script you write should express something you want to say. It doesn't have to be ultra-deep or philosophical. Make sure you don't preach. Instead of a cool idea for a movie, think about what value or insight you want to share in the telling of your story. Movies entertain, yes. Absolutely. But that doesn't mean you can't have your cake and eat it, too. Will this movie matter? Will it be relevant?

What if this will be the last screenplay I ever write?

Please take this in the most non-narcissistic way: make something that lives on after you are long gone.

Chapter 2

SIGNATURE DISHES
Genres

*"I don't choose genres as the element,
but the material itself is the element,
then I'll decide what genre I need."*

—Ang Lee, director, *Life of Pi*

If you love watching a certain movie genre, you can write it! If you respond emotionally to it, you are capable of creating it. Don't mix a bunch of genres in one singular screenplay. None of that *Se7en* meets *When Harry Met Sally* with a splash of *Elf*. A screenplay is not a Vegas buffet. It is a three-course meal with laser focus. While I love Vegas buffets for the variety, I must resist in writing a buffet.

You may feel drama is in your wheelhouse. But you might surprise yourself with skills in crafting suspense thrillers and horrors. When writing your first three to four screenplays, it's good to explore different genres. Once you land on the genre you enjoy writing and that spotlights your best work, stick with it. If that horror script gets traction, you may want to follow up with another horror or thriller. But don't go polar opposite and write a romantic comedy. I'm sure you can write a fantastic rom com. But imagine this. If you were a patient who needs brain surgery, would you hire a psychiatrist to operate on you? I mean they are a licensed M.D. after all, and did some surgery rotation during their residency many moons ago. Don't know about you, but I'd feel much better to have the specialist who is current in brain surgery to do this job.

MOVIES TO STUDY

Below are movie genres minus subcategories. I am focusing on primary ones. Feel your screenplay is a combination of genres? Pick one only! *Decide.* A horror is a horror. It may have comedic tone, like *Scream* and *Get Out.* But horror is at its core.

For each respective genre, I've prescribed a key element that's particular to it along with loglines of three movies with exemplary narrative structures. I've included correlating worldwide box office numbers, showing its *capture of the global audience.* When the term box office is used, please don't dismiss it as commercialism. It is simply a reflection of the mass audience it spoke to. Oscar nominees and winners as well as worldwide box office numbers are noted for your reference.

*Oscar nominee for Best Picture or Best Foreign Language Film
**Oscar winner for Best Picture, Best Animated Feature, or Best Foreign Language Film
Box Office Source: www.BoxOfficeMojo.com

ACTION
Which one or two major action sequences will end up in the trailer? They must be fresh and mind-blowing so that audiences will talk about them after walking out of the theaters.

Avatar (2009)
An ex-marine (Sam Worthington) is thrust into hostilities on an alien planet filled with exotic life forms. As an Avatar, he finds himself torn between a desperate fight for his own survival and that of the indigenous creatures.
Box Office: $2,787,965,087

***The Hunger Games* (2012)**
Set in a dystopian future where children are chosen as "tributes" and forced to compete in an elaborate televised fight to the death, a young woman (Jennifer Lawrence) volunteers to take her younger sister's place and travels to the Capitol to train and compete in the games.
Box Office: $694,394,724

***The Dark Knight* (2008)**
Batman (Christian Bale) takes on anarchistic mastermind known as the Joker who seeks to turn Gotham City to chaos.
Box Office: $1,004,934,033

ANIMATION
Why does this need to be animated? Envisioning the movie as animation isn't enough. What is it about the story, characters, and the world that live action special effects can't capture?

*****Coco* (2017)**
A 12-year-old boy is accidentally transported to the Land of the Dead, where he seeks the help of his deceased great-great-grandfather musician to return to his family among the living.
Box Office: $807,082,196

*****Up* (2009)**
By tying thousands of balloons to his house, an elderly widower sets out to fulfill his dream to see the wilds of South America and complete a promise made to his late wife.
Box Office: $735,099,082

*****Zootopia* (2016)**
An unlikely partnership forms between a rookie rabbit police officer and a fox con artist as they uncover a conspiracy involving the disappearances of savage predator inhabitants of a mammalian metropolis.
Box Office: $1,023,784,195

COMEDY

What is the heart? No matter how broad or slapstick they are, comedies need to tug at the audience's emotions. After the laughter, they need to feel that "awwww" at the end after the protagonist learns their lesson. Without that, it's nothing more than just a series of gimmicks. Shtick may help sell your script. But the actual paying audience won't buy into it.

*The Full Monty (1997, United Kingdom)

An unemployed steel worker (Robert Carlyle) rounds up his ex-colleagues to form a male striptease act that goes all nude for money in order to share custody of his son.
Box Office: $257,938,649

Home Alone (1990)

When an eight-year-old boy (Macaulay Culkin) is accidentally left behind after his family flies to Paris for their Christmas vacation, he has to fight off two burglars.
Box Office: $476,684,675

*The Wedding Banquet—Xi Yan (1993, Taiwan)

When a gay Taiwanese American man marries a mainland Chinese woman to please his parents and get her a green card, his plan backfires when the parents arrive in America to plan his wedding banquet while he hides the truth of his boyfriend.
Box Office: $23,600,000

CRIME

A sense of injustice or betrayal fuels the antagonist or someone in the inner circle betrays the protagonist.

**The Departed (2006)

An undercover cop (Leonardo DiCaprio) and a mole in the police attempt to identify each other while infiltrating an Irish gang in South Boston.
Box Office: $291,465,034

The Fate of the Furious (2017)

When a mysterious woman seduces a street racer (Vin Diesel) into the world of terrorism, his crew faces trials that will test them as never before.
Box Office: $1,236,005,118

**The Godfather (1972)

After the attempted murder of a crime family patriarch, the youngest son (Al Pacino) transforms from reluctant family outsider to ruthless mafia boss.
Box Office: $245,066,411

DRAMA

Whether it's divorce, separation, or death, a loss often sets up the premise or drives the protagonist.

***Departures—Okuribito* (2008, Japan)

When a young man (Masahiro Motoki) returns to his hometown after a failed career as a cellist and stumbles across work as a traditional Japanese ritual mortician, he is subjected to prejudice from those around him, including his own wife.
Box Office: $69,932,387

***Life Is Beautiful—La vita è bella* (1997, Italy)

A Jewish-Italian bookshop owner (Roberto Benigni) employs his fertile imagination to shield his son from the horrors of internment in a Nazi concentration camp.
Box Office: $229,163,264

**Rain Man (1988)

After a car salesman (Tom Cruise) attends his estranged father's funeral, he meets the autistic brother he never knew existed who has been left with their father's inheritance.
Box Office: $354,825,435

FANTASY

When building the world, rules need to be set up in the beginning for the narrative and the characters to navigate through. These need to be figured out thoroughly, but avoid long winded exposition in the movie itself.

**Crouching Tiger, Hidden Dragon—Wo Hu Cang Long (2000, Taiwan)

In 19th century Qing Dynasty China, a warrior (Chow Yun-Fat) gives his sword to his lover to deliver to safe keeping. But when it is stolen, the chase is on to find it.
Box Office: $213,525,736

Harry Potter and the Sorcerer's Stone (2001)

When an orphaned boy (Daniel Radcliffe) enrolls in a school of wizardry, he learns the truth about himself, his family, and the terrible evil that haunts the magical world.
Box Office: $975,051,288

Pirates of the Caribbean: The Curse of the Black Pearl (2003)

A blacksmith (Orlando Bloom) teams up with an eccentric pirate to save his love from undead pirates.
Box Office: $654,264,015

HORROR

The worst fear you have or can ever imagine. Sometimes it is tethered to a haunting past.

*The Exorcist (1973)

When a teenage girl is possessed by a mysterious entity, a young priest (Jason Miller) tries to save her through exorcism.
Box Office: $441,306,145

Get Out (2017)
A young black man (Daniel Kaluuya) uncovers a disturbing secret when he meets the family of his white girlfriend.
Box Office: $255,407,663

The Sixth Sense (1999)
A child psychologist (Bruce Willis) tries to help a troubled, isolated boy who is able to see and talk to the dead.
Box Office: $672,806,292

MUSICAL
Characters initially trapped in a physical location or situation but ultimately escape out of it.

Enchanted (2007)
An evil queen forces a princess (Amy Adams) from her traditional animated world into the live-action world of New York City where she falls in love with a divorce lawyer.
Box Office: $340,487,652

The Greatest Showman (2017)
A visionary (Hugh Jackman) rises from nothing to create a spectacle that becomes a worldwide sensation, giving birth to show business.
Box Office: $434,993,183

La La Land (2016)
A jazz pianist (Ryan Gosling) meets and falls in love with an aspiring actress in Los Angeles while both are pursuing their dreams.
Box Office: $446,092,357

PERIOD

If it's a true story, identify which part will make it the most cinematic movie instead of trying to cover everything. How does this moment in history reflect modern times and social landscape? Why is this story relevant to the audience today?

**Gladiator* (2000)

When a former Roman General (Russell Crowe) sets out to exact vengeance against the corrupt emperor who murdered his family and sent him into slavery, he rises through the ranks of the gladiatorial arena to seek revenge.
Box Office: $460,583,960

Hidden Figures (2016)

A female African-American mathematician (Taraji P. Henson) serves a vital role in calculating NASA's first launch of astronaut John Glenn into orbit during the early years of the U.S. space program.
Box Office: $235,956,898

**Schindler's List* (1993)

A German businessman (Liam Neeson) saves the lives of more than a thousand Jewish refugees from the Holocaust by employing them in his factories during World War II.
Box Office: $322,139,355

ROMANCE

Our views on romance are intrinsic. What do you want to say about love? How do you see love? How does that tie into family, past or present?

A Star Is Born (2018)

A famous musician (Bradley Cooper) helps a young singer find fame, even as age and alcoholism send his own career into a downward spiral.
Box Office: $429,823,201

** *Titanic* (1997)

A seventeen-year-old aristocrat (Kate Winslet) falls in love with a kind but poor artist aboard the luxurious, ill-fated RMS Titanic.
Box Office: $2,187,463,944

While You Were Sleeping (1995)

A hopeless romantic and transit token collector (Sandra Bullock) is mistaken for the fiancée of a coma patient.
Box Office: $182,057,016

SCI-FI

Reflections of human reliance on or ignorance of science, e.g., technology, environment, cloning, alien life forms, etc.

* *Arrival* (2016)

A linguist (Amy Adams) is recruited by the military to communicate with alien lifeforms after twelve mysterious spacecraft land around the world.
Box Office: $203,388,186

Transformers: Dark of the Moon (2011)

Autobots and Decepticons battle to possess powerful technology from their homeworld that had crashed on Earth's moon.
Box Office: $1,123,794,079

The Terminator (1984)

When a cyborg is sent back in time to assassinate a waitress whose unborn son will lead humanity into a war against the machines, a soldier (Michael Biehn) from that war is sent to protect her at all costs.
Box Office: $78,371,200

THRILLER

"Things aren't always what they seem." The reveal of a secret or a dark past haunts a character's guilt and vulnerability.

**The Secret in Their Eyes—El secreto de sus ojos (2009, Argentina)

A retired legal counselor (Ricardo Darin) writes a novel hoping to find closure for one of his past unsolved homicide cases and his unreciprocated love with his supervisor.
Box Office: $33,965,279

Se7en (1995)

A retiring detective (Morgan Freeman) partners with his rookie replacement to hunt a serial killer who uses the seven deadly sins as a motif in his murders.
Box Office: $327,311,859

**Silence of the Lambs (1991)

A young FBI trainee (Jodie Foster) seeks the advice of an imprisoned psychiatrist and cannibalistic serial killer to apprehend another serial killer who skins his female victims' corpses.
Box Office: $272,742,922

Chapter 3

FIRING UP THE STORY
Protagonist and Antagonist

"Acting is not about being someone different.
It's finding the similarity in what is apparently
different, then finding myself in there."

—Meryl Streep, actress, *Sophie's Choice*

T he movies people keep going back to over and over again don't necessarily have the most exhilarating plots. If you break down the plotlines of your favorite flicks, they are mostly unexciting and unmemorable. In *Planes, Trains, and Automobiles*, a self-centered businessman (Steve Martin) is determined to make it home to Chicago from New York for Thanksgiving. It's not the most riveting movie storyline. While the audience *find themselves* in his motivation, it is the dynamic clashes of him and clumsy travel companion Del (John Candy) that make the movie so memorable. The protagonist and antagonist are the critical ingredients of your story. They are the engine that stokes the fire and attention of the audience. Without well-crafted ones, the movie will taste flat no matter how ingenious the narrative is.

THE MOVIE HERO

The term here isn't restricted only to superheroes in spandex suits. It includes heroes without the "super." American movies foster the belief that you can do anything and reach any goal. The audience believes in the power of that. It's the regular guys who step up to do heroic actions. Tom Hanks made a great career playing that *regular* fella next door who does extraordinary things, such as playing an insurance lawyer who negotiates for a spy exchange in *Bridge of Spies* or a school teacher turned captain of a battalion in *Saving Private Ryan*. They do actions that defy the social norms. Our civilized daily lives render us powerless. That's why we admire that empowerment. Children feel invincible and can do anything. They're completely unstoppable. But the older you get, the more afraid you become. There are more consequences as adults. We have obligations. We are aware of risks. We have more at stake. Adults avoid being their true selves because they care too much of what others think. The movie hero is active in a way the audience *wishes* they could be. Modern civilizations groom people to be passive in order to maintain unison. That's why if we all acted the way protagonists do in real life, it would be anarchy!

When watching the protagonist in that dark theater, we root for that mirror version of ourselves. We wish we had their courage. We pine for their belief in themselves. *Something we wish we could have.* Or still had. Something we wish we hadn't lost. There is a whole cottage industry of self-help gurus and seminars to help empower us. It reflects the current state of how lost most of us feel.

ONE PROTAGONIST—ONE GOAL—ONE REASON

There is only *one* protagonist in every movie. They are the main driving force. There may be a "buddy" who is part of the team with significant screen time, but the one protagonist driving the story must be clearly defined. Just like there is only one protagonist, there can be only *one goal* throughout the entire movie. That one goal must have a major stake transfused into it. This needs to be established early on, within the first 30–35 minutes or Act One to be exact. The protagonist must fight for something. That's the kernel. This strong, clear goal is very prevalent in American films that the global audience consumes and is *used to*. It's their expectation.

The protagonist wants to achieve the one goal at this story entry point in their life. This is what lays down the plot and structure, producing the narrative of the movie. And the wide audience identifies with it. This cannot be a general wish. In *Taken*, Bryan Mills (Liam Neeson) fights to save his teenage daughter in Europe from beginning to end. It never sidetracks. The reasoning behind his action resonates with the audience. You would do anything to save your daughter. But as a practical and law-abiding citizen, you don't take matters into your own hands. You let the law enforcement professionals do their thing. We admire the hell out of Liam Neeson for going to Paris solo and infiltrating a human trafficking ring to find his daughter. This is why the audience cares and cheers him on! We *wish* we could be like him and say "fuck it." The protagonist fighting for their son, daughter, husband, or wife. Sound familiar? Yes, it does! In *Die Hard*, John McClane (Bruce Willis) fights to save his hostage wife. In *Lethal Weapon*, Murtaugh (Danny Glover) fights to save his kidnapped daughter. In *Salt*, Salt (Angelina Jolie) fights to save her husband. You rarely see the protagonist fighting to save a second cousin or uncle—unless that uncle is a father figure. All their goals are clichéd . . . yet universal.

SO WHAT? THE STAKES

In real life, decisions are made with several reasons informing them. But in movie life, there is *one reason only*. The audience needs to be aware of the stakes involved. Meaning, what would happen if the protagonist doesn't accomplish the goal? If they have nothing to lose and there are no consequences if they fail, the audience will have *zero* interest in the character and their journey. The critical question to pose is "so what?" *So what* if travel book store owner Will (Hugh Grant) in *Notting Hill* doesn't declare his love for movie star Anna (Julia Roberts) at the very public movie press conference at the end? He will lose the love of his life! Now that's something us hopeless romantics can all get behind. *So what* if Miguel in *Coco* doesn't find his great-great grandfather in the Land of the Dead? Then he can never return to the Land of the Living. *So what* if in *Back to the Future*, Marty McFly (Michael J. Fox) doesn't get his parents to fall in love? Then he will be wiped from existence!

Notice the simplicity of the stakes and how they're tied to the protagonist's action? Here are two more examples to drive it home. Gaz (Robert Carlyle) strips for money in *The Full Monty* so he can share custody of his son. In *Mrs. Doubtfire*, Daniel (Robin Williams) disguises himself as a female nanny so he can spend time with his children. This relatable motivation of wanting to be with their children is the buy-in for the audience.

ANATOMY OF THE PROTAGONIST

Upon their first entrance in the movie, here are three protagonist traits to show right away.

SKILLS

Introduce the skill set that will be used at some point to help achieve their goal. This is often done with exposition of their job. Thus, the profession you give your protagonist can't be arbitrary. It must be logical to the narrative story.

FLAW
Thematic or literal, take your pick. Think of those in your life. Coworkers, family, and friends. What trait of theirs do you find annoying or even detrimental to your relationship?

THE NEED
The protagonist is not aware of this, but the audience is. This is tied to their flaw. Although the audience sees it from the start, the protagonist realizes the need typically near the end of the movie. Audiences root for the protagonist to redeem this flaw.

THE ARC
Arc is the satisfaction of the protagonist's need—which is essentially the redemption of their flaw. When they change, it creates an emotional satisfaction, and we love them for it. Here's one that you've seen lots of times. And it works! The selfish, career-focused parent neglects their child. The need is recognizing that spending time with their children is more important than their career. In *Liar Liar,* Fletcher (Jim Carrey) neglects his son to win a court case to make partner at his law firm. In *What Women Want,* Nick (Mel Gibson) is estranged from his teenage daughter while he is working to win an advertising contract for his promotion. Both protagonists awaken to realize their kids are more important than their profession. It's simple and universal, no matter what country you are from.

Clichés are clichés because they work.

Movies revolve around the character's arc. It's always prevalent in American films but not necessarily present in movies from around the world. *Arc is what makes the movie.* Most non-American movies fail to connect with a global audience due to the protagonists not changing! They are perfect heroes from beginning to end. Or they are so flawed that redemption is impossible. If there is no room for change, there is no desire for the audience to root for them. In real life, people *don't change* most of the time. We go and watch movies for:

Hope.

And that hope is really about the protagonist's relationship to the people around them. We don't want to watch "perfect" protagonists. No one relates to that.

WHOSE STORY IS THIS?

In a buddy movie, it's challenging to figure out who the protagonist is since all the characters share similar goals. It's simple. The story belongs to the character who is actively driving the story and who has the most to lose.

Rush Hour **(1998):** Lee (Jackie Chan) is the protagonist, *not* Carter (Chris Tucker). Lee is the one who is active to save the kidnapped daughter of the Chinese Consul. He is the one responsible for her, whereas Chris Tucker has nothing to lose in this investigation.

Lethal Weapon **(1987):** Murtaugh (Danny Glover) is the protagonist, *not* Riggs (Mel Gibson). Danny Glover is the *active one* investigating the drug dealers who are responsible for the overdose death of his Vietnam War buddy's daughter. The bad guys eventually kidnap Danny Glover's daughter, too! His personal stakes are huge versus Mel Gibson who is suicidal and has nothing to lose. The protagonist has *everything* to lose!

Silence of the Lambs **(1991):** FBI trainee Clarice (Jodie Foster) is the protagonist. It's *not* Hannibal Lecter who is helping her profile the serial killer. She is the *active* one tracking the killer. If she doesn't find him in time, an innocent young woman will die.

ONE ANTAGONIST—ONE GOAL—ONE REASON

Just as there is only *one* protagonist in a movie, there is only *one* antagonist. They are the singular force whose goal counters *directly* against the goal of the protagonist. Do not split your antagonists into different characters. Have *one* who is all powerful. The antagonist of a great movie ignites the whole narrative plot. They are the roadblocks that the protagonist must overcome at every turn.

A movie without a strong, sophisticated antagonist is mediocre at best.

No matter how much screen time the antagonist has, they must be multidimensional. They can't be like "Dr. Evil" from *Austin Powers* or those old Bond villains where they were evil for the pure sake of being evil. Antagonists can't easily be discarded as stupid. Give the same love and care in constructing the antagonist as you do for the protagonist. They must hold their own set of values that are justified in *their minds.* The difference here is the audience is wired to the protagonist! They are experiencing the journey through their lens. They embody the audience. In the antagonist's perspective, they aren't "bad." Their worldview is rationalized— just in a warped way. The more you can loop the audience into the antagonist's mindset, the more impactful the conflict can be in the narrative.

"YOU AND I ARE NOT SO DIFFERENT"

Heard a variation of this line spoken by the antagonist before? Or "I've finally met my worthy adversary"? The most effective antagonists are those who are essentially the demented version of the protagonist. They are at the core the same character! In *Se7en*, Detective Lieutenant William Somerset (Morgan Freeman) is meticulous and logical just like the serial killer John Doe. Both dedicate their lives to rid the world of evil. Except John Doe is psychotic in brutally murdering those who commit sins and making an example out of them. In *Zootopia*, the protagonist rabbit police officer Judy Hopps (Ginnifer Goodwin) and the villain sheep Assistant Mayor Bellwether (Jenny Slate) are both physically smaller and have disdain for predator mammals stemmed from past humiliations. But Bellwether goes extreme in her evil plan to kill off all predators. In *Aliens*, Ripley (Sigourney Weaver) takes on a protective mother role with the sole survivor young girl just like the Alien Queen Mother is protecting her children. The Alien Queen Mother will kill off every human to do just that! *Zootopia* and *Aliens* are two completely different movies, but both antagonists have similar parallels.

The antagonist must share certain attributes with the protagonist. In *Star Wars*, Luke Skywalker (Mark Hamill) is a Jedi just like Darth Vader. And to drive it home even closer, they are father and son! We may not relate to what it's like being a Jedi. But we sure can connect to the dynamics between a father and son. Go to the extreme with the antagonist. Don't hold back. Enhance their attitude and skills. Blow them up to be larger than life. Make the audience feel in the beginning of the movie that the protagonist is going up against all odds. No way can they beat the antagonists. Johnny (William Zabka) of the Cobra Kai from *The Karate Kid*. Apollo Creed (Carl Weathers) from *Rocky*. Thanos (Josh Brolin) from *Avengers: Infinity War*. If it feels too exaggerated, it's always easier to tone it down later.

You must get into the mindset of the antagonist and/or villain when creating the character. See the movie through their perspective. Whatever they are doing, it's justified. Approach the antagonist as you would with the protagonist. Only then will the fire and conflict between the two feel authentic. All Commodus (Joaquin Phoenix) wants in *Gladiator* is his emperor father's love and approval. Who can't relate to that? Instead, his father prefers Russell Crowe over his own blood to succeed him. Joaquin Phoenix deals with his daddy issues in a psychotic way, but is rightly justified in his mind. The antagonist reminds the audience of *what's at stake* for the protagonist if they don't accomplish the narrative goal set out at the beginning. If Russell Crowe doesn't kill Joaquin Phoenix, then his family would have died in vain. And corruption of Rome will continue with senseless murders and injustice.

The antagonist *must be* a character. They don't have to be human. They can be an alien, monster, robot, or beast. It *cannot* be an "institution" or that the antagonist is the protagonist "themselves."

One movie to quickly dispel the common misstep of wanting to create an internal antagonist within the protagonist is *Fight Club*. Tyler Durden (Brad Pitt) is the antagonist within the Narrator (Ed Norton). The twist near the end is that they are in fact the same character with a split personality. But notice how Brad Pitt is manifested into a *physical character* the audience sees instead of an intangible thing?

EXCEPTIONS, *YES!*

There are always exceptions to everything. In both *Cast Away* and *The Perfect Storm*, there are no antagonists who are characters. Nature is what's keeping the protagonists from getting home. But in ninety-nine percent of critical and memorable American movies, the antagonist is manifested in the form of a character.

VILLAINS

There is a distinction between "antagonist" and "villain." Sometimes, the antagonist can also be the villain. If there are both, the antagonist is the one in action while the villain has less screen time. The villain is the one who the protagonist must destroy literally or figuratively by the end. In *The Town*, FBI Agent Frawley (Jon Hamm) is the antagonist chasing after Doug McCray (Ben Affleck) to bust him for the bank robberies. But the real villain is Fergie (Pete Postlethwaite) who controls Ben Affleck and is the one who had caused his mother's death by feeding her dope.

***Star Wars* (1977):** Darth Vader is the active antagonist battling Mark Hamill and the rebels throughout the entire film. He wants

CRAZY SCREENWRITING SECRETS • LIN

Mark Hamill to join the dark side as it's the only way they can be reunited as father and son. But Mark Hamill's goal is to destroy the dark side. The villain is the manipulative Emperor who orders Darth Vader to carry out the destruction of the rebellion.

Minority Report (2002): Department of Justice agent Danny Witwer (Colin Farrell) is the antagonist chasing to arrest Chief Anderton (Tom Cruise) for committing a future crime. But the villain twist reveal is Tom Cruise's mentor Pre-Crime Founder and Director Lamar Burgess (Max von Sydow) as the one who framed him.

The Fugitive (1993): U.S. Marshal Gerard (Tommy Lee Jones) is the antagonist hunting down the convict Dr. Kimble (Harrison Ford) for the murder of his wife. But the villain twist reveal is Dr. Kimble's medical colleague who had orchestrated the killing.

WHAT ABOUT DRAMAS AND ROMANTIC COMEDIES?

It's easy to construct the antagonist in sci-fi, horrors, thrillers, and action movies. But what about dramas and comedies? Remember, the antagonist is the character who is actively and directly preventing our protagonist from achieving their goal.

They are not necessarily "bad."

Rain Man (1988): Tom Cruise wants to get to Los Angeles to seek custody of his autistic brother Raymond (Dustin Hoffman) for control of his inheritance. He is a constant roadblock to Tom Cruise from reaching Los Angeles through his eccentric fear of flying and refusal to travel on the freeway.

Forrest Gump (1994): Tom Hanks wants the love of Jenny (Robin Wright). It's that pursuit for her heart that takes him to all the places in the world. But Robin Wright is the antagonist as she refuses to love and commit to him.

Notting Hill (1999): Hugh Grant wants to win the love of Julia Roberts. She doesn't fully give her love.

Now that you've got a handle of protagonists and antagonists, below is a simple tool to help you create them for your own script.

BIOGRAPHY

You should know the backstory of your protagonist and antagonist thoroughly. Even if elements don't show up in the movie, the context fuels their behavior. It paves the foundation for the audience to believe them. Write the biography for each in third person. Avoid describing mundane details such as height, weight, eye, and hair color. Those are great for novels. But they are a slow, wretched death for screenplays. Capture what defines them aside from physical traits—unless it is a handicap or is something that emotionally sculpted them. Pick very specific moment and circumstance in their lives that inform who they are *today*. What incident changed their life and values forever? Yes, it needs to be that dramatic! A girl loses her mother at age nine, and the step mother burns every photo of her birth mother. How does that shape the young girl as an adult? My grandmother lived to be 104. She recounted that traumatic, true moment with crystal clear clarity until her passing.

Here are a few questions to help you get started in the concise biography that's emotionally relevant to the characters. Consider their:

Biggest Fear: *What caused it? How has it affected them?*

Biggest Love: *Who? And what did that one moment feel like then and now?*

Biggest Loss: *What's the impact on this person today? How long ago was it?*

Write a biography for the protagonist and antagonist with the following format guidelines:

1. Half a page
2. Single-spaced
3. 12 pt. Times New Roman font

Why the format restriction if you are the only one who is seeing it? This helps you to write *concisely*. You should know the character on all levels, but you don't need to write out a 200-page biography. This half-page biography should be intentional, curated, and relevant to the protagonist in the juncture of their life depicted in the movie.

MONOLOGUE

Write a monologue in *their voice*. It could be an actual moment in the screenplay or it could not be. While they can speak to a specific character, don't have others interject or do any action. Be specific instead of giving a general, broad overview. Avoid talking about something we already know from the biography. Instead of rattling off in generalization about the horrors of war, monologue about the very last breath of a brother dying in their arms. Or that moment in *Rain Man* when Tom Cruise monologues to his girlfriend about his father leaving him in jail as a teenager and about his imaginary friend Rain Man.

Write a monologue for the protagonist and antagonist with the following format guidelines:

1. Half a page
2. Screenplay format
3. 12 pt. Courier font

If you create incredible characters, it will resonate with great actors. But the actors aren't the most important. No one involved in making the movie is. *Who is, then?*

The audience.

Period. They are the ones who the movie serves. The actor will embody the character and seduce the audience into believing in them. They are the vessel of the character's soul. The actor's ownership of that character is what taps into the imagination of the audience. The right actor will elevate it beyond your wildest dreams. It will stay in the audience's hearts long after the end credits roll.

Chapter 4

THREE-COURSE MEAL
Movie Structure

*"With a good script, a good director can
produce a masterpiece. With the same script,
a mediocre director can make a passable
film. But with a bad script even a good
director can't possibly create a good film."*

—**Akira Kurosawa**, writer and
director, *Seven Samurai*

As a kid, I used to get annoyed at my parents for staring at
me whenever I ate. As I became an adult, I realized that it
brought them so much happiness to see their children eat. Food is
how Taiwanese and Chinese cultures express love. I love eating. I
love cooking. It's how I show love to my friends and family. Every
word I write comes out of care for my loved ones.

MOVIES ARE OUR COMFORT FOOD

We consume stories by the way we eat. Look at how cuisines are
different from country to country! Sure, we eat the same basic food
groups. But they are all prepared and presented differently. After
all, this is about creating stories that capture the global audience.
The late chef and author Anthony Bourdain showed us how food

connects us all to humanity. God, I miss him. And although we eat differently, we all have the universal craving for storytelling. I believe with every conviction in my bones that movies are the most powerful connectors of human beings.

STRUCTURE, *NOT FORMULA*

The generalization of American films is that they are formulaic. Everyone seems to have heard about the mythical Three Act structure like it's some secret potion concocted by mad Hollywood scientists to ensure box office success, forcing all its filmmakers to follow blindly. Formula is a term that gets tossed around in association with "Hollywood" movies. But it's misguided. Instead of formula, think of it as *structure*. Instead of saying, "Oh, that's so formulaic," try saying, "Oh, that's so structured!" Structure is necessary. It's a narrative platform that organizes the characters in relation to the story.

Structure is the invisible seam that the screenwriter stitches the story together.

From the classic Aristotle to today's proclaimed screenwriting gurus, this is literally what movie structure is . . . wait for it . . .

Beginning. Middle. End.

Ta da! Groundbreaking stuff! Why does the world watch American movies as their main consumption of cinema? These are characters who don't speak the same language and don't even look like them! Global audiences read subtitles for American films because they are *good movies*, structured in the way they are used to. The quick blame on Americans not caring for foreign films is their unwillingness to read subtitles. That's not all true. If the structure is not recognizable, the audience has to work harder to "get" the narrative. That's why American audiences don't like to watch foreign films. It's too much hard work to "get it."

This is not to say American movies always rule the box office of other countries. China's local production of *Wolf Warrior 2* 战狼 *2* is the highest-grossing movie in that territory, ever. It made over $800 million at the Chinese box office. $800 whoppin' million! You read that right. China's first sci-fi movie *The Wandering Earth* 流浪地球 became another blockbuster, earning $700 million. Based on Hugo Award-winning Chinese author Liu Cixin's short story, it is China's second highest grossing movie. The top Hollywood tentpole in China is *The Fate of the Furious*, which scored $392 million. It pales in comparison. Outside of China, *Wolf Warrior 2* 战狼 2 earned $4 million while *The Wandering Earth* 流浪地球 made $7 million. *The Fate of the Furious*, however, made over $1 billion outside of the United States.

So *why* the Hollywood domination? For over 100 years, the American film industry has been going non-stop. Neither politics nor war disrupted its volume of production and its infrastructure, whereas film industries of most other countries were crippled due to war, politics, and social unrest. The American film industry has never shut down. Thus, it is the world's most mature and systematic film industry. The constant supply of films from Hollywood became the ones that the global viewers became accustomed to. As a result, the worldwide audience subconsciously expects high quality content presented in the Hollywood narrative structure. Let's simply call it *global structure*. One can attribute the high production value to Hollywood's large budgets for its success around the world. But it's also important to note certain Chinese movies with Oscar winning designers and stars match those budgets of Hollywood's tentpoles. Yet, they don't resonate globally like American films

It all goes back to what's on the page.

AVOID WRITING LIKE A CHINESE BANQUET

I love traditional Chinese banquet dinners. I love it like a good Las Vegas buffet. The variety of different dishes that I can eat to my heart's content is my happy place. My stomach is always satisfied after such a feast. But one of the biggest missteps in creating the screenplay for a global movie is approaching it like a "Chinese Banquet." If you have ever been to an authentic, traditional Chinese restaurant, there are several dishes served on that "Lazy Susan" table to be shared amongst the guests. Main course dishes can range from spicy Sichuan beef, steamed whitefish, lettuce shrimp wraps, braised pork to Peking duck all served without a specific order. It's equivalent to mixing genres, tones, and storylines sporadically throughout a movie script. A new writer is often tempted to put in every character, idea, and dialogue into their script as if it will be the only one they'll ever write. While it can be personally satisfying, it might be overwhelming to the audience.

WRITE LIKE A THREE-COURSE MEAL

Notice in Americanized Chinese restaurants, there are often lunch and dinner specials where each person eats their own *one main course* with a side of egg roll appetizer and soup to compliment it? The heart and soul of your movie is the main course. The appetizer, paired wine, sides, and dessert are there to support and enhance it. None should ever overtake it. At a proper western restaurant, you wouldn't be eating miso fish at the same time as a beef taco. It may be tempting at some point in your script to tag on some story idea, character, or irrelevant dialogue line from your creative vaults. *You must resist this at all costs*—unless it is an essential tissue of the narrative. As you start working on pages, check that each scene you write is consistent, focused, and *organic* to the entire screenplay.

What happens when you throw out structure and invent your own original, groundbreaking structure? The chance of connecting with a significant audience will diminish astronomically. Foreign-language films that scored global box office and critical acclaim (nominated or won Oscars) such as *Secret in Their Eyes* (Argentina), *Life Is Beautiful* (Italy), and *Departures* (Japan) are structured in the way laid out in this book. While talent and perspective cannot be taught, the structural craft can be. Once you have mastered structure, you can go to town with your own unique and creative narratives. But until you become the next auteur like Quentin Tarantino (*Pulp Fiction*) or Paul Thomas Anderson (*Magnolia*), embracing the structure will carry the story to the world.

RECIPE

Not every hamburger is created equal. A Wolfgang Puck burger will taste differently than a Big Mac. Think of structure as the recipe. There are basic elements that go into a hamburger such as two halves of a bun and a beef patty in between. Structure is the burger. And there are endless, creative ways you can enhance the burger. Certain restaurants will add something extra like cheese, onions, spreads, bacon, special spices, guacamole, toasted buns, egg, etc. Then there is the quality of the meat, how well or rare it's cooked, marinated or not, how many slices of tomato, and so on. That's *originality*. If you don't care for structure, what it means is that when the audience orders a hamburger, you serve them a fried catfish sandwiched in between a pancake and pizza slice. That sounds very original and has never been done before in a burger. Maybe a select few customers might appreciate the originality. But the gigantic majority will revolt. You are not giving them what they expect. When ordering a hamburger (structure) you *want* the basic elements when eating one. Beef patty in between the buns. And all the creative culinary infusion is what makes one "the best burger I've ever had." For screenwriting purpose, it translates to: "That's the best movie I've ever seen!"

BLUEPRINT

You probably hear this screenplay analogy all day along. Most new writers are anxious to hit the pages because they "see" the movie in their heads. So they start writing away without a specific outline. But what they "see" is usually just set ups or certain scenes and moments. You wouldn't start construction of a building or high rise without a proper blueprint with every detail thought out . . . *or would you?* This is a $100 million building! You can't simply just show up to the construction site and break ground without planning out the entire foundation—floor by floor, wall by wall, room by room.

What happens if halfway through construction, you realize you forgot to lay down the proper piping and electrical outlets? Or miscalculated measurements? Then what? You are already halfway through construction. You've burnt through significant resources. The right thing to do is tear down what you have built and start from scratch. Yikes! This will frustrate and stunt your writing. Most likely, you will be inclined to work around the faulty construction that you have already poured blood and sweat into. You will attempt to salvage it. It may appear on the surface to be okay, but that screenplay will become a flimsy, imperfect movie with flaws that can fold like a house of cards.

AMERICAN NARRATIVE STRUCTURE

There are several iterations on movie structure by countless books, blogs, and teachers. Ultimately, they are all conveying more or less the same thing through their perspective. The next few chapters will offer another iteration from my perspective. I will refer to *Rain Man* often. Do yourself a favor and watch it if you haven't before. This extremely *low-concept* movie about a man's road trip with his autistic brother made $355 million worldwide! And that was in 1988. Zero special effects. No action set pieces. Sure, it's got two movie stars in it. But when was the last time a star studded, small drama connected with such a large global audience? It's a simple movie with near-perfect sculpture of characters and narrative.

The Three Act structure is not formulaic. All the creativity is in the scenes you incorporate within this structure of which the audience of the world are *used to*. What happens if you throw structure out the window? The audience will be in confusion, disrupting what they are accustomed to. That's a bad thing. They will reject the world you created and will not buy into it. You may not be interested in writing Hollywood blockbuster movies. But this structure applies to "smaller" movies, too! *Sideways*, *Nebraska*, and *Brokeback Mountain* are all critical and box office hits. They prescribe to the same structure found in "bigger" movies like *Transformers* and *The LEGO Movie* . Yes, you can surely break away from structure. But it's critical you know it well before you do. Writers Quentin Tarantino (*Inglorious Basterds*) and Darren Aronofsky (*Black Swan*) are known to do just that. But you can bet they've mastered structure before reinventing it. There are exceptions to films that veer away from the patterns of this structure. But you must *learn and know it* before you can break away.

EVERYONE'S GOT A MOVIE IDEA. SERIOUSLY. *EVERYONE.*

From your barber to your accountant, anyone who watches movies thinks they've got an idea for one. But most don't have a *story*. Just an idea. It's easy to jump right into writing pages. Might as well jump into the abyss! Steam will most likely run out around twenty-five pages if you're lucky enough to even hit that mark. To avoid that, a writer must do the preparation work to structure the entire movie in an outline. Structure helps reduce the gap of what you want to say and what the reader takes in from the page.

Chapter 5

RECIPES
The Step Outline

*"For the great doesn't happen through impulse
alone, and is a succession of little things
that are brought together. And the great isn't
something accidental; it must be willed."*

—**Vincent Van Gogh**, painter, *The Starry Night*

tory is the recipe. When you write a script without following a recipe, you have no idea what dish you'll end up with. You start cooking. But then have to stop and go out to buy ingredients you need due to not having prepared. This will add frustration and delay to the process. Yes, there are screenwriters who don't outline. Their approach is discovering their story and characters as they write. Only a handful of top professional writers can get away with it. They are brilliant and very experienced. But for us mere mortal craftsmen, isn't it better to work out the plot in the outline instead of juggling to find the narrative in midst of script pages after months of hard work? If your process is to never outline, give it a try. And the outline I'm suggesting is only *one* page! Not eight. Not twelve. *One!* You just might love it. Think through the entire movie in terms of plot before you type "Fade In." If not, there is a very high chance of writing yourself into a corner. Your structure will be far from sound. You can wing it for a high school English essay. But you can't wing it for a screenplay that will be the basis for a $100 million picture.

TITLES

Don't start your screenplay with "Untitled." It can be a working title that only you share with yourself and no one else. It's only something for you to see. It can be a temporary placeholder. Keep it simple. Don't beat yourself up in trying to come up with a catchy or an awesome literary title. Start with a single word or two that reflects your story. Don't know where to start? Try with the location or character(s). Check out these mostly one-word titles!

LOCATIONS
Casablanca (1942)
Chicago (2002)
Dunkirk (2017)
Jurassic Park (1993)
Philadelphia (1993)
Titanic (1997)
Waterworld (1995)
Zombieland (2009)
Zootopia (2016)

CHARACTERS
Amadeus (1984)
Avatar (2009)
Braveheart (1995)
Gandhi (1982)
Gladiator (2002)
The Godfather (1972)
Rocky (1976)
Salt (2010)
Wolf Warrior 2 (2017, China)

These are Oscar Best Picture nominees, winners, or box office champions. Not bad company to be in. They are all very simple, capturing the essence of the movie. Anything is better than *Untitled*.

It's like having a baby and calling them "Unnamed" until they turn 18.

TAGLINES

Taglines are a must! Again, this is just for you. Once your movie gets that glorious greenlight to production, the marketing team of the studio will come up with ingenious ones. But in the meantime, create one for yourself. You are a writer! You can do it. This helps you articulate the kernel of the potential theme. Keep it simple like the title. While your screenplay is specific, the most effective taglines are broad. They are catchy and universally applicable. Want ideas? See posters of your favorite American movies. Or if you are into foreign films, consider the ones that were Oscar winners or nominees of Best Foreign Language Film. Below are a few to get you inspired.

American Beauty (1999): Look closer

Crazy Rich Asians (2018): The only thing crazier than love is family

Creed (2015): Your legacy is more than a name

Fantastic Beasts: The Crimes of Grindelwald (2018): Who will change the future?

Fifty Shades of Grey (2015): Lose control

Green Book (2018): Inspired by a true friendship

Platoon (1986): The first casualty of war is innocence

A Quiet Place (2018): If they hear you, they hunt you

Ready Player One (2018): A better reality awaits

Wonder Woman (2017): The future of justice starts with her

Zootopia (2016): Welcome to the urban jungle

POSTER

This is my favorite part of the prep. Making a poster of the movie you are about to write! This is your visual instinct for the story.

If you or a friend is savvy with Photoshop, make an actual poster design with your ideal actors. It can also be a simple image, artwork, or photograph that captures the tone, style and emotion of your movie. Another alternative is to cut out images from magazines and color print-outs from the internet. Then put together a collage on legal sized paper of your visual feelings of the movie. It's good fuel for creativity. Most of all, it's a lot of fun! Takes you right back to the arts and crafts of childhood. You can tape it on the wall next to your workstation as a visceral connection to the cinematic world you are writing in.

STEP OUTLINE

You've created the protagonist and antagonist. Gotten a poster mock-up of the movie with a title and tagline. Now you are *almost* ready to construct a one-page outline of the screenplay by breaking down your movie into *steps*. Think of these steps as discs in your spine. Discs are tough ligaments that hold the vertebrae of the spine together. Each step represents *three minutes* of the movie or three pages of the screenplay. It is written in only a single line. And no more. Remember, the step does not necessarily represent a scene. Avoid details of scenes in this outline. The step is a simple and concise summary of what happens in those three minutes. This is your road map. When driving cross country, you would plan out your routes for the most efficient course. That's what you should do for your screenplay. Don't worry; you are not locked into this. Your step outline may evolve as you go along. Just like your handy GPS will suggest alternative, shorter routes should you hit traffic or accidents. As you discover new directions, the step outline will evolve. But be sure to revise it immediately on the step outline to see if those changes affect other steps.

The entire outline document should be no longer than one page. Format guidelines below:

1. Single-spaced
2. Each step is one line only (can write in fragments)
3. Number each step
4. 12 pt. Times New Roman font

Before step-outlining your own movie, first use this format to break-down an American film that is similar in genre to the story you are planning to write. If it is a foreign-language movie, it must be either an Oscar Nominee or Winner for Best Foreign Language Film. Once again, each step represents literally three minutes of the movie. Type out the step outline. Step one would be three minutes. Step two would be six minutes. Step three would be nine minutes. Below is a quick sample from *Se7en.*

1. Retiring Det. Somerset meets his rookie replacement Det. Mills for a one-week transition
2. Somerset listens to metronome to fall asleep. Mills meets Somerset at a crime scene.
3. They find a dead man in a bowl of food with his hands bound. Victim ate himself to death.

After you have outlined all the steps of the existing movie, you can track the plot all on *one page.* These steps are not necessarily scenes. It streamlines the narrative. It's not exciting to look at. In fact, it's boring! If it's exciting, then you are doing something wrong. Take a good look. Can you see the spine? Maybe outline another similar movie. Doing this will really help you understand the genre you are writing and get your mindset in on it. You are no longer just a patron who eats the dishes. You are now the chef who must figure out the ingredients and study how the taste is invoked.

If eagerness propels you to write screenplay pages before having completed the outline, you will ultimately be slammed by a concrete wall of frustration. Most writers feel the creative nature of screenwriting gives them license to just make it up as they go along. Most professionals outline. Most novices don't.

The joke is, if you walk into a Hollywood-centric coffee shop in Los Angeles, you will most definitely see a handful of writers working on their screenplays. If you ask how many feature-length screenplays they have written, most of them will probably say *none*. But they've got the first twenty pages of five different screenplays. How come they didn't finish them? They probably got lost and frustrated in the script and gave up. The reason for giving up nine out of ten times is the lack of outlining. Or not outlining *every step* of the entire movie. It's easy to figure out the first twenty minutes. Most people who watch movies will have an idea for the set-up. But Act Two, the body of the movie, is the hardest freakin' part to crack! It's like building the Great Wall! Okay, not that hard. But it sure does feel like it sometimes. There is more suffering conjugated in scripting of Act Two than any other part of the process.

Part Two

KITCHEN IN THE MADHOUSE

Screenplay Construction

"Stop thinking about writing as art. Think of it as work. If you're an artist, whatever you do is going to be art."

—Paddy Chayefsky, screenwriter, *Network*

Chapter 6

APPETIZER
Act One—Whet the Palate

*"When a film is about everything, it's
hard for it to be about anything."*

—**Terry Rossio**, screenwriter,
Pirates of the Caribbean

When you walk into a restaurant, the ambiance and décor set up the culinary experience you are about to have. A Michelin two-star-rated Spago and franchise chain Olive Garden will whet your palates with the appetizer, preparing you with a sensation of what is to come. While these are two polar opposite restaurants, there is consistency in what the diners expect in their meals at the respective establishments.

THE FIRST BITE

When you meet someone for the first time—whether it is a romantic potential, a new friend, or a coworker—you will most likely form an opinion of that person within the first ten minutes of meeting them. The first taste of food at a restaurant sets your impression of how the rest of the meal will be. If the appetizer is fantastic, the main course and dessert will most likely be as well. However, if the starters taste horrible, you can bet the rest will be equally bad.

The same goes for audience and the first ten minutes of the movie.

As well as for the readers of your screenplay. Agents, managers, producers, directors, actors, and executives will form an instinctual opinion based off the first ten pages. Having read hundreds of screenplays, those opinions are often spot on.

FIRST BITE (1–10 MINUTES)

Who is the protagonist? While the protagonist doesn't have to be introduced right in the opening scene, they must make their entrance by the *very latest* within ten minutes into the movie. What are their skills and flaws? Not only that, there needs to be a hint of explanation to empathize with that flaw here at the first bite.

TEXTURE

A good opening scene of a movie establishes:
1. **Tone**
2. **Style**
3. **Pace**

Within the first ten minutes, the audience should get a strong grasp of the protagonist and their:
1. **Skill**
2. **Flaw**
3. **Need**

Once all of the above have been established, they must be consistent throughout the entire screenplay.

Rain Man's tension-laced opening scene clocks in at three minutes. Tom Cruise is introduced as the owner of an exotic car dealership that is teetering on going under. His *skill* is selling and lying. His *flaw* is selfishness. He is disconnected from his work staff and his girlfriend, who are supposedly the closest people in his life. We get the sense he *needs* to become selfless and connect. Wow! All that in three minutes! This is a character drama. But it sure sets the story in motion fast. In the two scenes that follow, Tom Cruise learns that his estranged father has passed away and left him nothing in his will except for a car. The humanistic reason for his flaw is being left in jail for two nights when he was only fifteen years-old as punishment for taking his dad's car without permission. As a result, he ran away from home after that.

ACTION-ADVENTURES

Open with an action scene within the first ten minutes. In *Raiders of the Lost Ark*, Indiana Jones (Harrison Ford) steals a gold idol and races out of a booby-trapped temple as a giant boulder rolls after him! It's got flashes of comedy and an unforgettable action set piece. Elements include treasure, fear of snakes, and skill with a bullwhip—all of which pays off later on in the movie.

COMEDIES

Tickle the funny bone with a humorous set piece that revolves around the protagonist. In *There's Something About Mary*, Ted (Ben Stiller) has his private parts stuck in his zipper when picking up Mary for the prom.

DRAMAS

Introduce the protagonist where we immediately grasp their skills and flaws. This is typically showcased through their profession. In *A Star Is Born*, Jack (Bradley Cooper) is good at performing country music at a sold-out concert. His flaw is alcoholism and substance abuse.

THRILLERS

Hooks with a crime or thrilling scene that seduces the audience in its opening. In *A Quiet Place*, a young boy is killed by a creature due to the sound that his toy made.

THE CRAZY SITCH (17 MINUTES)

Crazy Sitch—as in the Crazy Situation! We all have encountered them. But we as the practical, fearful human beings run away from it at all costs. But protagonists take them on. Crazy! They will say *yes* and risk it all.

Movies are about crazy decisions. This is the central hook of American movie trailers that sets the premise. If it's the norm, why would the audience be interested?

Remember that crazy sitch when I flew in from New York to visit my wife at her company holiday party in downtown Los Angeles and high-tech terrorists took everyone hostage? *Die Hard.*

Or the crazy sitch when I first met my girlfriend's white, creepy parents at their house in the remote woods where it got all awkward because I was African-American? *Get Out.*

And who can forget the crazy sitch when the world's most famous movie star kissed me in my apartment? *Notting Hill.*

All these moments happen literally at 17 minutes into the respective movies. *It's that on point.* Don't believe me? Watch your favorite movie that's a critical hit with the Oscars or was a box office sensation. Subtracting credit sequences without dialogue, the Crazy Sitch will usually hit smack at 17 minutes, give or take a minute. Everything is relatable and normal up to this point until our protagonist comes across that—

Crazy sitch!

Every Crazy Sitch happens at 17 minutes into the movie, roughly page 17 of the screenplay.

Rain Man **(1988):** Tom Cruise meets Dustin Hoffman, the autistic *brother* he never knew he had at the mental institution.

The Wizard of Oz **(1939):** Tornado hits black and white Kansas, transporting Dorothy (Judy Garland) and her house to *Land of Oz* in Technicolor.

Back to the Future **(1985):** Michael J. Fox meets Doc's (Christopher Lloyd) invention, "You made a *time machine* out of a DeLorean?"

Arrival **(2016):** Louise (Amy Adams) and Ian (Jeremy Renner) team up and arrive at the *space ship* to decode alien language.

FULL STEAM—SINGULAR GOAL (25–35 MINUTES)

This is when the protagonist *decides* to act upon the crazy situation back at the seventeen-minute point. They are going *Full Steam* on this one-way track to achieve that single goal throughout Act Two. The audience also must be aware of what is at *stake* to enable their sympathy. This is the action plan for the entire movie. It will be the most impractical decision you and I would *never* make. But the protagonist would! Keep in mind, the goal is an intentional, narrative one. It's *not thematic*! It's *not theoretical*! It has to be tangible.

Rain Man **(1988):** Tom Cruise is going *Full Steam* to bring Dustin Hoffman to Los Angeles in order to get custody of him for his inheritance. The stake? His car business is about to fold unless he gets this money to save it. Driving cross country, he's got a week to make it in time.

Se7en **(1995):** Morgan Freeman is on *Full Steam* to catch the serial killer before he finishes his planned murders based on the seven deadly sins. Stake? More innocent victims will die unless he stops the killer. It's a one-week countdown. Seven days, seven sins, seven murders. Genius.

The Fugitive **(1993):** Harrison Ford kicks in *Full Steam* to find the one-armed man to prove his innocence. The stake? He will go to prison for a crime he didn't commit and the bad guy will get away with his wife's murder.

Ready Player One **(2018):** In *Full Steam*, Wade races *backwards* and wins the first key. Now the goal is to win the two remaining keys in order to find the Easter egg and own virtual reality OASIS. The stake? The evil CEO of online gaming corporation IOI will find it first and make OASIS a dark world.

In real life, we would suppress this crazy inclination and *not* go Full Steam. A young woman in 1912 would not give up marrying into a life of riches by following her true love with some poor artist she had a fling with on a ship like in *Titanic*. An enslaved, ex-Roman general would not fight in a bunch of gladiator tournaments so he can avenge the murder of his family by killing the emperor like in *Gladiator*.

Don't be afraid to spell it out literally of what the set-up is. The Full Steam has to be crystal clear to the audience so they will be along for the ride. If they are still wondering what the movie is about after thirty-five minutes have passed, the audience will check out.

PRESSURE COOKER

It always seems to be twenty-four hours, three days, or seven days. It adds pressure to the narrative pressure cooker. It works all the time. The *Mission: Impossible* franchise thrives on time locks. No matter how many times we've seen that bomb countdown devise used, we are all on the edge of our seats. Think of how tense you feel when you are late for something. Or stuck in traffic and feeling helpless being unable to reach your destination *on time*. We operate on time locks every day of our lives. Getting to jobs, classes, and meetings on time. When something delays us, tension escalates. The earlier you can plant the ticking clock, the better. Ideally within the first thirty-five minutes, if not earlier.

METAPHOR

This isn't something the audience will catch onto and dissect like a literary critic. But if there is an object or location you feel can visually serve as the vessel of the movie's theme, the crowd will subconsciously feel satisfied. In *Rain Man*, Tom Cruise drives his father's prized Buick, which caused the bitter estrangement as a teenager from his father he never saw again. Throughout the movie, Tom Cruise and his newly acquainted autistic brother Dustin Hoffman are on a cross country road trip in the very same Buick. It rekindles the past, and he gets closure with his late father by the end of the movie. You can also *discover* the metaphor as you write and then simply go back and steep it through the script.

Chapter 7

MAIN COURSE
Act Two—Savory Climax

"The journey changes you; it should change you . . .
you take something with you.
Hopefully, you leave something good behind."

—**Anthony Bourdain**, chef and
author, *Kitchen Confidential*

Now we are really moving. This is the *action* of the decision made at end of Act One. This is the hardest act to write. Anyone can write Act One and Act Three. But Act Two is where the real craft comes in. It's what holds the movie together and is critical to sustain the audience's imagination.

FORMING THE TEAM

American movies are hero-centric. But the heroes all have help. Although they may take the lead, there is always a buddy or team supporting them. Look at all the super hero movie franchises with their teammates. *The Avengers. Justice League. Guardians of the Galaxy.* Every protagonist has at least one partner. In rom coms, there is always that best friend confidant who serves as the sounding board. Humans have a desire to connect and thrive in a community. Even Tom Hanks in *Cast Away* had Wilson the volleyball!

ALL IN—MIDPOINT (50–65 MINUTES)

The protagonist goes from passive to *active*. Up until this point, the protagonist is *reactive* to the obstacles rather than being *active*. Once the protagonist turns active and takes initiative, they are *All In*. There is no turning back, emotionally or literally.

This is also the point when the protagonist and the antagonist are both on an *even playing field*. In an action movie, it's when the protagonist is proactive in using skills and smarts to accomplish their goal instead of just reacting to the actions of the antagonist. They are one step ahead for the first time. In dramas and romance films, this is when the protagonist and antagonist are both vulnerable and form a *genuine connection*. Sometimes it's sex in romance movies. Or it can be a moment when both share and feel *mutual vulnerability*.

***Rain Man* (1988):** At the motel, Tom Cruise is *active* in putting the bed next to the window just how Dustin Hoffman prefers it. This is in contrast to prior scenes when Tom Cruise was only reactive to him freaking out about his bed. Immediately after, Tom Cruise realizes Dustin Hoffman was his imaginary friend Rain Man. They both are in sync, singing a song from childhood *together*. Tom Cruise pieces together that his father sent Dustin Hoffman away to the institution, fearing that he might hurt him. The father did this out of love for Tom Cruise. He is emotionally *All In*.

***The Wizard of Oz* (1939):** After she meets the Wizard, Judy Garland is literally *All In*. In order for him to help her go home, she has to retrieve the Wicked Witch's broom. While she has Tin Man, Scarecrow, and Lion, Judy Garland is *active* in leading this mission.

***Se7en* (1995):** Instead of waiting for the next victim to show up, Morgan Freeman is *active* and illegally buys information from the FBI on library books checked out about Dante's *Inferno*. Armed with the address of a potential suspect, he and Brad Pitt go to John Doe's apartment, leading to a shootout confrontation. Literally, he has gone *All In*.

***A Star Is Born* (2018):** At backstage of his concert, Bradley Cooper is *active* and declares his love for Ally (Lady Gaga). With his encouragement, she sings her original song solo to the crowd, overcoming her insecurity. They are now at equal footing as artists and lovers. Emotionally, he is *All In*.

LIVE OR DIE (90–100 MINUTES)

This is the *lowest* point ever in the entire movie. End of Act Two. This is when the audience gets that sinking feeling in the pit of their stomachs. Here, the *singular goal set up in Act One is achieved!* The protagonist almost kills or neutralizes the antagonist and/or villain. So why is it the lowest point? The protagonist must do something more to redeem their flaw, *satisfying* their need. *Figuratively or literally*, the audience is high on anticipation if the protagonists are going to *Live or Die*.

Here is when most people would simply give up. The stakes are too great. Odds are overwhelming. Made it all this way to only face this monstrous defeat. They feel powerless. Fears overtake them. Here, the audience is the most emotionally vulnerable for the protagonist. It's when they feel most emotionally vulnerable for *themselves*. This is the point of where "real life" would end . . . on a *low point*. It's the quitting time moment. Heck, in real life, we wouldn't have been crazy enough to go on this ride to begin with.

But in movie world, the protagonist *lives*, overcoming that lowest point. While they may physically die, they *live* out of the selfless sacrifice for the greater good.

Think of every romantic comedy where the couple splits up for good (*Live or Die!*) near the end of the film. But in Act Three, the protagonist swallows their pride and chases after "the one," declaring their love—usually in a public place. We love romantic comedies even though the ending is obvious before the movie starts. But we go and watch it anyway! In life, romantic relationships are usually left unresolved. We seldom end up with "the one." This predictable Act Three fulfills that desire and courage to go against all practicality to be with their true love.

American cinematic stories and relationships are always resolved. They are rarely left open-ended. Life is already uncertain. Movies are where audiences crave resolutions and are rewarded with them.

That's why the world loves American films.

Rain Man (**1988**): The doctor who controls the inheritance offers money to Tom Cruise, giving him exactly what he wanted from the start. But now, Tom Cruise wants custody of Dustin Hoffman out of his own selfish need for family instead of doing what's best for his brother. And that is to be back at the institution for proper care.

Live or Die: Will Tom Cruise do what's best for his brother and let him go, or remain selfish by holding on to him?

Wizard of Oz (**1939**): Judy Garland retrieves the Wicked Witch's broom so the Wizard of Oz will send her home. But turns out the Wizard is a fraud and has no magical powers.

Live or Die: Will Dorothy get home to Kansas or be stuck in the Land of Oz?

Se7en (**1995**): Morgan Freeman captures the serial killer when John Doe surrenders himself. But there are still two unaccounted bodies out in the desert.

Live or Die: Will Morgan Freeman recover the remaining bodies and solve the case?

A Star Is Born (**2018**): Back at home, Lady Gaga lies to alcoholic and drug addict Bradley Cooper that her concert tours are cancelled. She is staying put. It's what he wanted. But she is giving up her potential and artistry.

Live or Die: Will Bradley Cooper kill himself to *free* her?

Chapter 8

DESSERT
Act Three—Satisfaction

*"I can't get no satisfaction, I can't get no
satisfaction, 'cause I try and I try and I try . . ."*
—The Rolling Stones, rock
band, *Out of Our Heads* LP

The Rolling Stones sure got it right. In mortal life, we try our hardest to get satisfaction. In that quest, we are disappointed most of the time. But in cinema life, that's where satisfaction is promised! When does this happen? Act Three. Something that will put a smile on your face and instill hope as you float out of the cinema. While the goal set up in Act One is reached already, the protagonist reverts back to their flawed self. This is when they must *arc*. Change! Here, the world needs to end in a better place before the credits roll. It cannot be the same or worse. If a storyteller insists on making the movie end like "real life," then it's like:

Not getting to be together with "the one"!

Not saving the life of your loved one!

Not resolving estranged relationships!

Not going the distance after working so hard against all odds!

The end must satisfy the audience. Period. No way around it. Sweet closure. Like the perfect dessert at the end of a gastronomic three-course meal.

HOLLYWOOD ENDING

Whether it's an indie art house movie you are writing or a commercial blockbuster, consider writing an ending that is *satisfying*. It doesn't have to be "happy" per se, however it absolutely needs to be satisfying or the audience will hate you when they walk out of the theaters with an ending that's a punch in the gut. Say goodbye to word of mouth! They've invested in the emotional roller coaster ride and trusted you to leave them on a high note instead of sending them off the rails, crashing to the cement ground. *Power of Film* author Howard Suber coined it simply, "We watch movies to compensate for what's lacking in our lives." People feel unsatisfied most of their lives. It's plain sadistic to take the audience on this journey and not give them a sense of renewed hope.

Can you imagine if Tim Robbins in *The Shawshank Redemption* got caught during his escape after his seventeen years of perseverance in digging that tunnel? And spent the rest of life in jail, while Red (Morgan Freeman) hung himself like his predecessor Brooks, who couldn't adjust to life outside of prison? No! You'd be furious! It's probably more realistic, but beyond *dissatisfying*. During production, the original ending was simply Morgan Freeman riding the bus to see Tim Robbins in Zihuatanejo just like in Stephen King's novella. But we never *see* them reunited! After this long saga, the audience deserves to see them together. Ultimately, the studio paid for the extra filming costs to shoot the reunion scene. No dialogue exchanged here. All we needed to see was them finally free and being together on that beach they had *hoped* for all this time. It was the test audience's favorite scene. It *earned* the emotional elation and satisfaction.

The protagonist's journey must change the world for the better than when they started at fade in. Sure, they can die. But they must have made the world better or have inspired someone, a community, or even an entire nation who will continue that good work. In *A Quiet Place*, Lee Abbott (John Krasinski) sacrificing his life to save his family isn't exactly a happy moment. But it leads to the survival of his wife, son, and daughter who figures out how to defeat the creatures. We are satisfied from the assurance they and others will live on without having to hide in silence anymore. In *The Sixth Sense*, Malcolm (Bruce Willis) realizes that he has been dead this entire time! It's sad to know there is no chance he can be with his wife. The audience is satisfied, watching him accepting the reality and finally letting go. His wife is able to move on. He has helped Cole (Haley Joel Osment) psychologically, enabling him to use his gift of seeing dead people to help them transition.

Rain Man (1988): During the pre-custody hearing scene, Tom Cruise *arcs* by telling the truth for the first time. He does what's right for Dustin Hoffman by letting him go and reside back at the institution with proper psychological care. And for the first time ever, Dustin Hoffman initiates touch by leaning his forehead on Tom Cruise's. These two men had no family at the beginning of the movie. And now they do.

The Wizard of Oz (1939): Dorothy clicks her shoes and is back in Kansas. Here, she *arcs* by appreciating all her relatives whereas before, she was bored and took everything for granted. This echoes the theme of "There is no place like home."

Se7en (1995): Morgan Freeman was initially retiring because he was sick of the evil in the world and felt he made no difference. He was giving up. At the end, he *arcs* when he decides to stay on the force, echoing the words of Ernest Hemingway that the "world is worth fighting for."

Here are the ending imageries from three Oscar winners of Best Picture. All are global hits.

Braveheart (1995): As he is executed, William Wallace (Mel Gibson) reunites with his dead wife in the afterlife.

Gladiator (2000): After Russell Crowe dies at the final gladiator fight, he reunites with his dead wife and children in the afterlife.

Titanic (1997): After old Rose presumably dies, we see youthful Kate Winslet reuniting with her true love Leonardo DiCaprio in the afterlife.

We don't care that these are similar endings, do we? We feel so good and *satisfied*.

Movies are about hope.

And it's our obligation as writers to give that to the audience.

INTIMATE STORIES

The same goes for smaller, indie films. It's satisfying to see Chiron (Trevante Rhodes) and Kevin (André Holland) unite as adults and address their unresolved childhood romance at the end of *Moonlight*. They have closure. In *Leaving Las Vegas*, Ben (Nicolas Cage) drinks himself to death. Even though he dies, Sera (Elisabeth Shue) leaves her abusive pimp and prostitution as a result of her romance with Nicolas Cage. It's satisfying to see Elisabeth Shue start a new life. Both of these endings are seasoned with satisfaction.

POPCORN FLICKS

In tentpole studio films, endings are fueled with direct, satisfying, and yes, super happy "*Riding off into the Sunsets*." Princess Diana (Gal Gadot) destroys the super villain Ares (David Thewlis) in the final fight in *Wonder Woman* and saves the world. Bruce Willis saves his wife and blasts the villain Hans Gruber (Alan Rickman) off the building to his death in *Die Hard*. The antagonists in blockbuster movies are big, bad, and powerful. That means the ending needs a gigantic punch that's worthy of the IMAX 3D ticket price that moves the audience to cheer out loud.

YOUR OUTLINE

Now that you've got a grasp of the Three Acts, you are finally *ready* to do the step outline for your own screenplay. Remember the step outline of an existing movie you did in Chapter 5? Review it and underline the *Big Four* steps introduced in the previous two chapters:

1. Underline the ***Crazy Sitch*** (17 minutes) in Act One [step 5 or 6]

2. Underline the ***Full Steam*** (25–35 minutes) in Act Two [steps 8 to 12]

3. Underline the ***All In*** (50–65 minutes) in Act Two [steps 17 to 22]

4. Underline the ***Live or Die*** (90–100 minutes) in Act Three [steps 30 to 33]

A feature-length screenplay should be around 105 pages, which translates to thirty-five steps. Once you are done, revise it thoroughly before typing any screenplay pages. *Do not* leave blank steps thinking you'll figure it out in the script pages when you get there.

No. Negative. Never.

This leads to writing yourself into a corner. If you can't figure it out now, there is no guarantee you can figure it out later. Plotting it out fuels the viability of the movie narrative.

A single line only for each step. Not even one word over! You can write in fragments. Each step is equal to three pages of your screenplay. And be sure to underline the *Big Four* in your outline as well. If you feel it's impossible to fit three minutes of summary on that single line, review the step outline you broke down for an existing movie. See? It's possible. Should you get stuck at some point along the way, check out other movies in the genre you're writing. Study the correlating moments you are stumping on. Perhaps they can inspire solutions for your narrative.

Don't worry if this takes a while to get the hang of. The more films you watch identifying these four key structural scenes, the more it will sink in. Yes, it's only four! Like the number of legs on a chair and table. It will ensure the stability of your movie structure. When watching American films from now on, turn on the *subtitles* and pay attention to the *timecodes*. With technology making this a breeze with a click of a button, there are no excuses! The more intentional you are in identifying them, the more it will sink in. Before you know it, this will all be second nature.

COMMENCE!

You've done all the prep. It's time to open that new script file in the industry standard Final Draft software.

A good script isn't enough. It has to be great! Whatever it takes to get it right. *Getting it right for you.* Don't worry about the final movie product. There will be development and rewrites that follow to get there. Here is your shot to get the script as you see the movie before it goes to others who will help shepherd it into a movie playing at a theater or a streaming device near you.

Chapter 9

PRESENTATION
Organic Action and Dialogue

*"The fundamental of anything as a director
is material, material, material—script,
script, script—once you have the script,
everything else is straightforward."*

—Ridley Scott, director, *Gladiator*

The screenplay isn't something you read like a novel. Most people haven't been exposed to this bastardized storytelling format that's a jumbled form of poetry, prose, and play. It is a funky hybrid of literature, source code, and ground plan. Here are some tips and techniques to make storytelling pop in this medium for the readers.

FORMAT

Formatting is strictly standardized in the American film industry. It's a sign of an amateur if the script isn't written in the standard Hollywood format. It was created over 100 years ago and is still used today. Don't try to format this yourself. Buy the software Final Draft and avoid loads of frustration. If you are a student, the company offers incredible educational discount. It supports several languages, including Chinese, starting with Final Draft 11.

Each page roughly represents one minute of the screenplay. The font is 12-point Courier. Script format has very specific margins. Unlike most fiction novels, the action and description in screenplays are always written in the present tense. The movie is unfolding in real time. That's why the screenplay must reflect that.

SCENE HEADINGS

A screenplay is composed of scenes. The heading will inform the reader if the scene is interior INT or exterior EXT. The location name follows after, ending with Day or Night.

```
INT. NATALIE'S BEDROOM — RANCH — NIGHT
```

WRITING ACTION AND DESCRIPTION

The amount of time it takes to read the action and description should reflect the actual screen time. Think of it like tweeting. The word limit in tweets forces you to use as few words as possible to express the most. Or better yet, think of it like writing a telegram in the old days where each word *costs money*! Let's see how much you can save.

ACTION

Give the highlight of the action. Avoid writing every single blocking. That's the director's job. If the character grabs a beer from the fridge, write exactly that!

```
Spencer grabs the beer from the fridge and
chugs it.
```

Instead of:

```
Spencer rises from his chair, walks over
```

```
to the fridge and opens the door. Then he
reaches for a beer and closes the door
before heading back to his seat. Opens the
beer and chugs it.
```

The reader assumes he will have to do all that to get the beer. Unless Spencer trips and breaks his nose against the fridge door, there is no need to track his action beat by beat. Write action that reflects the actual pace.

DESCRIPTION

When describing a location, do it in one sentence if you can. Fragments are welcome if they help make it concise. When describing a crappy apartment, just write:

```
Crappy shoebox apartment with no windows.
```

Instead of:

```
There are no windows in this 200-square-
foot studio apartment with peeling paint.
It is decorated with cheap, mismatched
furniture and worn-out yellowing carpet
from the 1970s. There are no heaters and
air conditioning units.
```

This is a script. Not the great American novel! Crappy shoebox apartment will insinuate that the furnishing and décor will suck. Let the production designer do their job.

Concise writing is everything.

Author Stephen King puts it best, "Good description usually consists of a few well-chosen details that will stand for everything else." So. Good. That's why he is Stephen King. His articulation is on point. The best book on writing of any kind is *On Writing* by Stephen King. No question. Buy it as soon as you finish reading this book. Actually, order it now.

SCENE CONSTRUCTION

Each scene should exist because of the previous scene before. If the scenes are interchangeable, there is an issue. Don't just insert a scene arbitrarily, even if you've spent weeks crafting it. If it doesn't fit organically, then you must discard it. Each scene has to move the story forward and reveal something about your characters. A great scene serves multiple purposes. But filling the page with irrelevant dialogue to hit the page count is definitely not one of them. A scene must be efficient in developing the story and character relationships.

NEVER AGREE

Make it hard for the character to get what they want. Going against the opposite is what laces the scene with conflict and makes it interesting. When both characters agree, the scene is over. They may share the same goal but should have opposite approaches. Look at all the buddy-buddy movies. They often share the common narrative goal but within the scenes, they have conflicting ways of achieving them. Thus, it creates tension, conflict, and *irresistible chemistry*.

Let's say a couple sits down on their first date. One says, "I love black coffee." And the other jumps in, "I love black coffee, too!" End scene. It's over. Done. In real life, that's the ideal. We want to find points of common interest to avoid conflict in the potential romantic relationship. However, in movie life, that would be dull. This goes for every scene. The characters can come to an agreement at end of the scene—but *only* at the end.

LOCATION, LOCATION, LOCATION

Locations for your scenes can't be random. Don't just plug in a cool ferret breeder farm you just visited on vacation. They need to be logical to the characters. In *Notting Hill*, movie star Julia Roberts asks Hugh Grant to meet her after their serendipitous kiss. Instead of setting the location at some café so they can chat without distraction, she invites him to her hotel in the midst of media interviews. That's a much more interesting and integral location! Julia Roberts is in London to promote her movie and her schedule is packed. This press junket adds tension and comedy as Hugh Grant poses as a journalist interviewing her as the publicist pops in and out. In between, they sneak in precious exchange and an arrangement for their first date. The secrecy heightens the chemistry, making us smile through it all.

Avoid coffee shops and cafes like the plague. No, actually avoid it like black pudding! They will end up as talking heads unless that cafe is extremely critical to the development of the narrative and character on hand. Yes, there are exceptions like the café scene in *Pulp Fiction*. But guns also come out blazing later on to make it much more interesting than them pouring out exposition dialogues over a cup of coffee.

DIALOGUE

The first test is to read the dialogue and distinguish who the characters are without reading the names. One thought per dialogue line. *One thought*. Don't tackle several thoughts. It will just come across as exposition dump from the writer versus what the character's intention is. Never repeat anything in a dialogue. No back and forth. There's more freedom to do this in a play. But in a screenplay, it's a huge sin. The dialogue can't be repetitive of what's already shown in the action. A character says, "Get out of my house!" There is no need to add 'she screams at him' in the action. The dialogue punctuated by the exclamation mark pretty much tells us she is screaming at him. Try to have no more than three lines of dialogue per character at a time. In comedy, it's around two lines. This is not law. But if you are writing a bunch of five-line dialogue chunks, back track to take another look at how to express that more efficiently.

INTERACTION

Every line a character says, the other must respond. It can be in the form of dialogue, action, or a reaction. Each dialogue exchange must reveal something about a character. Every. Single. Exchange. *Exaggerate the character's reaction.* This is a movie! Intensify the reactions as long as they remain true. If it's too out there, you can always dial it back. If a scene is stale, ask yourself what does each character want in this scene? Approach it as if you are the actor playing the role. At a job interview, what's the motivation of the candidate? *Convince* the interviewer to hire them! Every word and action from the candidate in that scene is motivated by the desire to get hired. What is it that you want in that very moment? And what if you don't get it? *So what?* Writers should take an acting class. No need to go to a fancy one. Junior colleges or local university extension classes offer them for minimal tuition. That is one of the best ways to help make your dialogue writing shine! Focusing on one character instead of juggling several will add multi-dimensionality whenever you write a character in any given scene. For those of you who are more on the introverted side, taking those classes can enhance your interpersonal and pitching skills in a room when going up for those great writing assignments.

DISTINCTION

To distinguish dialogue so they don't all sound like you, assign an appropriate one-word personality to specific characters. *Ambitious. Insecure. Compassionate. Eager.* And so on. Another way is to cast the actors in your head. They can be voices of a coworker, relative, or friend who embodies that persona. Or they can be famous actors who can capture the soul of your characters.

SUPPORTING CHARACTERS

Every character who has dialogue needs to have a specific trait. Even the actors who have only one line of dialogue. They are people, too. The more attention you pay to every detail, the more authentic the overall narrative will be. Instead of naming single occurrence characters like COP #1 and WOMAN #2, give an adjective instead of a number. Like JARHEAD COP, ALPHA DUDE, SPUNKY LADY.

Dovetail your characters. Don't insert a new character to serve only a single purpose. Combine those characters as much as you can. This will help with the flow.

NO SCOOBY-DOO REVEALS

A typical reveal in *Scooby-Doo* is when they pull off the mask of a non-threatening character, and they turn out to be the villain with little to no set up. Zero warning! While audiences love allies who betray, it can't be random. They have to be peppered in throughout the narrative in order to earn the payoff. In *The Sixth Sense*, Bruce Willis flashes back to the moments that set up the realization that he is dead. It *earned* the twist and that's why it was incredibly satisfying to the audience—$672 million worth of *global* satisfaction.

Chapter 10

EMOTIONS
Moving Stories
Before Moving Scenes

*"Our primary function is to create an emotion
and our second job is to sustain that emotion."*

—Alfred Hitchcock, director,
North by Northwest

*C*ast Away screenwriter William Broyles, Jr. wasn't stuck on an
island for several years hanging out with a volleyball named
Wilson. But he did write with the "emotions" that he knew. Upon
Tom Hanks's return to civilization near the end of *Cast Away*, he is
completely estranged from the place he fought so hard to stay alive
to return to. William Broyles, Jr. wrote with the emotions he knew.
It was how he felt when he returned home from his tour of duty in
the Vietnam War. That parlayed emotion was so powerful that it
moved the audience. This truth was from the core of his soul.

We watch movies to feel.

And our feelings are heightened through loss, love, and disconnection. It's no surprise that many of the memorable films are about
disconnection. *Cast Away* captures the heart of that. But there is
hope. While Tom Hanks is pretty much severed from civilization

during all of Act Two, it is his connection with Wilson the volleyball that keeps him alive. Though Wilson is an object, we crave connection so badly that we believe in that friendship. When he loses Wilson at sea, we feel the audience's heartbreak through Tom Hanks's painful cries of love for it.

SCENES

When remembering our favorite movies, we feel the emotional scenes that struck a chord in us. Eager to write similar emotional scenes into our scripts, we make the common mistake of creating those scenes separate from the overall story. It's the story that has to be emotional and moving *first*. In a typical Asian melodrama, there will be stacks of heightened crying and shouting scenes that come out of left field without relating to the narrative. The writer and/or filmmaker desperately wanted to cram in an emotional scene, disregarding its relevance to the narrative and characters as a whole. This is reflected in many Asian movie trailers that feature emotional and dramatic scenes, but most fail to include the premise. The priority is placed on individual scenes instead of story. That endangers the cohesion of the entire movie. This works with Asian audiences because that's what *they are used to* in the consumption of their own films. That is also why those movies don't travel outside of their own territory in a significant way. It drastically contrasts with American movies where the trailer is essentially the Act One, which shows the *Crazy Sitch* in the first half and then teases with the best scenes through the second half of the trailer. When a movie places importance on moments rather than the overall story, its narrative will minimize the reach of a global audience.

EXPRESSION OF LOVE

Timeless stories are about love. Find as many unique ways of expressing this in your screenplay. Be vulnerable in how your characters love. The more afraid they are of love and intimacy, the better. The more emotionally exposed, the more your audience will sympathize and connect to them. Try it in your own life. Don't hold back when it comes to love. We are capable of it. Look at children. They never hold back. Life is too short to regret. Cast aside ego, pride, and logic. See what happens. Be bold with love.

Be naked.

We are more open to our honest emotions amongst strangers in a darkened theater than we are in our day to day lives. There is something beautiful about that.

Chapter 11

THERAPY
Digesting Notes and Rewriting

"The first draft of anything is shit."
—**Ernest Hemingway**, author,
A Farewell to Arms

Congratulations! You've finished the writer's draft! If this is your first feature-length screenplay, extra kudos. It's no small feat. In my book, you are a bona fide screenwriter by writing a 90- to 105-page script. Now, the real writing begins. With this being a collaborative medium, taking and processing notes is a large part of the screenwriting process. Welcome to therapy of *distilling notes* and applying what is helpful in making the screenplay you want to write as best as it can be.

TAKING NOTES

You will always get notes. *No matter who you are.* Oscar winners. Kajillion-dollar screenwriters. Digest the notes you receive. But do not apply them at face value. *Do not* take all the notes. If you do, the script will suck. If you don't take *any* of the notes, the script will suck *harder*. Your most valuable asset is your *instinct*. That's what talent is. As you carefully review all the feedback, only extrapolate ones that might potentially work for your story. Your decisions in taking and rejecting particular notes define your voice.

It is natural to feel emotional as you immerse in rewrites with armful of notes from your managers, agents, writer friends, executives, producers, directors, and/or actors. It's a tough job to assess which notes are helpful to the script you are writing. Don't dismiss the notes based on who they're coming from or for personal reasons. Most creatives in the industry are very smart. Instead of disregarding notes right off the bat even if it's light years away from what you are going for, *listen*. Listen thoroughly as if the note is coming from the mouth of your screenwriter hero.

The art of giving and receiving notes is a delicate one. While certain suggestions may not be perfect solutions, they often pinpoint a legitimate flaw in the story. The key is identifying the *intention* of the note. After going through the process a few times, you will formulate a system that works for you without driving yourself nuts.

Notes come from various perspectives. Sometimes they can be conflicting. It is rare for a room full of people to agree 100% about a movie no matter how much box office or critical accolades it has received. During this process, set aside the personal ego. Approach it from an *audience perception*.

SAFETY INSPECTION

When rewriting, be a safety inspector. Look for holes and flimsy structure. Be objective. Give it a thorough inspection to see if the framework holds. The following are a few elements to review.

RULE OF THREE

Each scene should not go over three pages. Four is sometimes the maximum. There are exceptions when scenes garner more pages. However, if you have several five-page scenes, you either trim it down or break them up into different scenes. Comedies tend to have two- to three-page scenes and are dialogue driven.

Keep each paragraph of actions and descriptions no longer than three lines. If a sequence demands longer chunks of descriptions (typically in dramas, action, and thrillers), consider breaking it up into separate paragraphs for pace.

ECONOMICAL

Page time reflects screen time. If a fight scene will only be ten seconds on screen, don't spend a whole page describing that action. Write only 1/6 of a page for it.

FRAGMENTS

It's okay to write in fragments for pacing, especially in action and comedy. But like anything, overdoing it will lose its effect.

KEEP IT LEAN

Avoid full pages of only descriptions without dialogue interspersed. Even in action sequences, you can punch in one-liners.

e.g., "Watch Out!" or "Stop him!" Find that fine balance of action and dialogue.

TONE

Maintain tone consistency throughout the script. If it's a comedy, write the action with humor. If it's an action movie, write with adrenaline and rhythm.

NO QUESTIONS AND ANSWERS

Avoid characters asking consecutive questions to another who replies with lengthy answers. This is how scenes end up being in the exposition black hole.

Each dialogue is about one thing.

CHARACTERS

If a scene is lacking certain energy and tension, ask what does each character want either literally or sub-textually in that specific moment. Keep it to one verb. Don't go off on a tangent.

Persuade her.
Hurt him.
Motivate them.

LOCATIONS

When the scene is stale, set it at *another location*. Make sure it's inherent to the characters and story. Brainstorming locations on where these characters would go or how they would act as *fish out of water* in an unfamiliar environment can help break you out of a rut.

EMOTIONS

While structure can be guided, no one can teach feelings. That is up to you. Good movies are *all* about feelings. It's the most critical ingredient in an effective motion picture. And the "movement of emotions" is what people will remember.

TABLE READING

Now that you've done the rewrite and safety inspection, it's time to hear the script out loud instead of it echoing just in your brain. Get your actor friends together. The smart ones who really get into characters. Make it a cold read. This way, you are getting first reactions just like that producer who is reading your script. What I love about this is the actors will zero in on their characters and track them. Any bumps or inconsistencies, they can bring it to your attention. The dialogue may sound awesome in your head. But if the actor keeps fumbling over the words, it's a good sign it needs reworking. If actors are hard to come by where you live, you must have friends who hammed it up on stage in high school or in college for fun.

FELLOWSHIP OF WRITERS

No matter what stage you are in your career, there is no better support than a writer's group. Not everyone needs to be working on a screenplay. It can be a play. Novel. TV pilot. As long as they are committed to telling stories, they'd be great. Meet once every two weeks. This valuable support consists of fellow writers who want you to succeed without agendas. What a gift this is! If you are in college, get into a writing workshop and find those writers you connect with. Even if you are out of school, there are extension courses available. Some even have real-time online classes. If you live in a town where you are literally the only person interested in writing, I'd recommend going to Austin Film Festival's Writers Conference. It is truly one of the best for screenwriters packed with panels. Attendees range from newbie writers to veterans. There, you just might meet a scribe in your neck of the woods who is passionate about storytelling like you! Now with technology, you can even do video conferencing for your writers' group. Forming that great group is a creative lifeline that can help get your work as best as it can be.

PERSPECTIVES

Screenwriters may *feel like* second-class citizens since nobody *sees* them writing. Everyone sees actors act, directors direct, and designers design. But the way I *see* it, writers create the only tangible property before the movie is made. They are the first ones to get compensated for their work. If the movie isn't greenlit for production, there is no full employment for the director, actors, cinematographer, producers, and crew. When the script doesn't get set up or is stuck in the unfortunate development abyss, writers can always write a *new* screenplay using nothing but white paper and black ink. They're the same exact tools used by Oscar winners *and* first-time screenwriters.

EAGER BEAVER

Don't set a ticking time clock for yourself. Time locks are great in screenplays. But not in your writing career. There is no hurry. Don't plot out a calendar of selling a number of scripts by an age benchmark. You will drive yourself crazy—in a *negative* way. Writing is a way of life. You need to be a writer. Keep writing the best material you possibly can. Work hard and persevere. It's what you *need* to do.

HAVE FUN

If the fun stops, unpack and figure out what's blocking that fun. Find the joy.

I'll confess.

Writing script pages can be *painful*. I'm definitely not one of those writers punching out words with orgasmic literary bliss every hour of every day. It's okay if you feel the same way!

So why do I do it? Creating a new screenplay is hands-down the biggest high I've ever had. And I chase that high with every new script. Kind of sick, right? But it feels so good. At the risk of sounding naïve, I truly believe a story can make a difference in the world. With that in mind, don't be so precious about the script. While it's important to listen to others, it is critical to fully trust your instincts and remove the ego. A tune-up of perspectives can go a long way in seeing the fun in every screenplay.

Chapter 12

PROCESS
Always Be Writing

*"Inspiration is for amateurs, the rest of
us just show up and get to work."*
—**Chuck Close**, painter, *John*

While novelists read novels to improve their craft, screenwriters should *read* screenplays instead of just watching movies. Especially for screenplays that you haven't seen the movie for yet. That's the best way to foster your style in the screenplay medium. Every year, studios release Oscar-contending screenplays online around award seasons. You can literally search the title of the movie and the key words "screenplay pdf." How many should you read? As many as possible! Read one professional screenplay a week to get started.

WRITING PROCESS

This is more about the *system* of writing. Aside from the nuts and bolts of actual writing, the process of outputting work is essential. Use a system that works for you to be prolific. It can help alleviate the daunting feeling of staring at the first blank page of a new script. It should take you no longer than twelve weeks to write a feature-length screenplay. Twelve weeks is also the expectation in the professional world to deliver. Everyone works differently. I balance a pipeline of three feature projects simultaneously in distinct phases.

Phase One: Concepts and Loglines
Seeds: Generate concepts and ideas.

Phase Two: Character Development and Step Outline
Prep: Develop protagonist and antagonist. Break story with step outline.

Phase Three: The Screenplay
Script: Upon finishing the first draft, move on to script pages of the next screenplay that was outlined in Phase Two. Hash out the story from Phase One into a step outline while creating new ideas.

This system helps keep everything moving like an assembly line.

TRAINING WHEEL SCRIPTS

These analogies driven you nuts yet? Here's more! Screenwriting is like building furniture. When I first put together a piece of Ikea furniture, it takes *hours*, and something always goes wrong! But those professional assemblers need only *minutes*. And it's flawless! Why? They've put together hundreds of them! All shapes and sizes. It takes practice to get great at it. Hundreds of hours, if not thousands.

I love that Picasso tale about napkin art. For those who aren't familiar with it, a patron at a Paris cafe asks Picasso to draw something for her on a napkin. He obliges and finishes it in remarkable speed. Upon handing it back to her, he asks for an obscenely high price. In shock, she uttered, "It only took you a minute!" But Picasso replied, "No, it took me forty years."

The more scripts you write, the better you get at it. Typically, it takes writing roughly four feature-length screenplays to get the hang of it. Oliver Stone (*Wall Street*) apparently has written over twenty. Scott Rosenberg (*Venom*) wrote ten before he made his first sale. These writers *needed* to be writers. By the way, Oliver Stone won an Oscar for writing *Midnight Express* before directing *Platoon*. Francis Ford Coppola wrote *Patton* before directing *The Godfather*. Damien Chazelle wrote *The Last Exorcism Part II* before directing *Whiplash*. For those of you who aspire to direct, screenwriting is a great way to break in. Just saying.

Don't jump into screenwriting with the lottery ticket mentality. As much as many books, blogs, and seminars will hype overnight successes, there are no short cuts. Nil. With every overnight success, there are over ten years of struggle behind it. But if you are willing to work hard, anything is possible.

WRITING SCHEDULE

The most common excuse for not writing is time. There is no time to write with a full-time job *and* family. These are *excuses*. If you believe that, you will never *schedule* the time to write. Approach writing as if you are clocking in for a job. It doesn't sound creatively sexy. You can't write only with inspiration. If you do, a prolific output won't be possible. Sometimes you can sit for five hours and write five words. But in another sitting, you might write fifteen pages! You need to write with *perspiration*. One prominent screenwriter was a former full-time lawyer with a family. To schedule his writing, he went to sleep at 10 PM but would wake up at 4 AM every morning and wrote for two hours without any distractions from his family or job. Then at 6 AM, he would get breakfast ready for his kids and send them off to school before a full workday at the law firm. He made it work.

While a feature-length screenplay is roughly 105 pages, there's a lot of white space! Let's say you write a three-page scene every day. Based on that schedule, you will finish a full screenplay in a month and some change. The hours before you have to go to work are ideal because that is when your mind is fresh. If getting up that early isn't an option, try writing after work. Instead of fighting traffic, write at the office or a café for a couple of hours. If you commute on a train, write on that long boring ride. That's how J.K. Rowling did it.

Write on a laptop. Write on a smartphone. Write on a notepad.

Do whatever it takes to make room for a writing life. Set deadlines. That's what professionals do. If not, then you won't ever be accountable.

SKELETON DRAFT

When you are falling behind deadlines and feel stunted in the writing as a result, try this *sculpting* approach. It is especially helpful if your perfectionism gets in the way. Based on the step outline, lay out all of the scenes in the screenplay with minimal, basic actions and descriptions like "Lucas sits," and "Ann kicks the ball." Write the essence of the dialogue. It can be on the nose. You can also write in brief prose of what needs to happen in the scene. By doing that, all the scenes of the entire movie are right in front of you! Psychologically, it fuels a sense of accomplishment. This process helps identify what scenes are essential or not. Once you've locked in all the scenes, you can go back and *sculpt* the details of action, description, and dialogue.

FEAR

Many writers fear the blank page. No matter how many scripts they've written, movies made, or awards won, there's a fear that trickles through the fibers with the start of a new project. Doubts percolate, wondering if they are any good or if they can top their last work.

It's that fear which keeps us doing our best writing.

If you aren't afraid, then the writing might not have the vulnerability to connect with its readers.

Part Three

LEAVING THE ASYLUM
The Writing Profession

"Scripts are what matter. If you get the foundations right and then you get the right ingredients on top, you stand a shot . . . but if you get those foundations wrong, then you absolutely don't stand a shot."

—**Tim Bevan**, producer and co-chairman, Working Title Films, *The Theory of Everything*

Chapter 13

WORKFLOW
From Screenplay to Theaters

*"I don't try to guess what a million people will
like. It's hard enough to know what I like."*

—John Huston, writer and
director, *The African Queen*

So how does it all work? After getting that feature-length
screenplay in top shape, what happens then? What is the journey of the screenplay to the big screen? What is the main difference
between the "studio" system and the "independent" system? Mel
Gibson's *Hacksaw Ridge*, Martin Scorsese's *Silence*, and Luc Besson's
Valerian and the City of a Thousand Planets were all independent
movies. An independent movie doesn't necessarily mean it has a low
budget or was made by unestablished directors. It just means the
financing doesn't come solely from the studio system.

But how is a production company different than a studio?

HOLLYWOOD STUDIO

This is a one-stop shop. The traditional majors include Disney/
Fox, Paramount, Sony, Universal, and Warner Bros. They have the
financial capability to buy scripts and finance the budgets of the
movies all on their own. Although nowadays, they often partner

with co-financiers like Legendary Entertainment, Skydance, and Chinese companies such as Tencent Pictures and Alibaba Pictures to minimize the risk as film budgets have skyrocketed. A studio has the distribution platform to market and release the movies. Major studios have some form of their own distribution entities in various international territories.

Do you sell a script directly to a studio, then?

Yes and no. The studio is the "buyer" of your script. They are the ones who pay the money to purchase your intellectual property. They are the owners of your script and ultimately the rights holder of the movie that is produced based on your script. But they have so many movies going on; they don't "creatively produce" the films. They have overall deals with select producers. This way, they can have the first look at the projects that the trusted producer wants to make. If they agree with the producer, they will buy the script for the producer to develop into a feature film. The owner of the script and movie is ultimately the studio. They paid for it. In turn, the studio pays for the producer's overhead for that first look privilege. Sometimes, a studio can also buy a screenplay or IP directly if they have a good working relationship with the writer and then assign a producer to develop it. There are also many stellar producers with great taste and track records who don't have deals but have strong relationships with studios. They can also bring in projects to set up.

PRODUCTION COMPANIES

Principal producers own the production companies. Typically, when we think producers, we think financing. That can be true in the independent film world where that's a big part of the job. But in the studio world, they don't have to worry about money while they have a deal. In the traditional sense, the producer's job is to identify properties like original screenplays, pitches, books, short stories, magazine articles, graphic novels, foreign films, amusement park rides, or toys that they see the potential of making them into motion pictures. The producer will submit to the studio for them to purchase or option the rights. This can sometimes add up to millions of dollars, including rights fees, screenplay commissions, and rewrites.

AGENT → PRODUCTION COMPANY → STUDIO

Once your original spec script is ready, the agent will take it out to potential buyers. Spec means speculative. That you wrote the screenplay on your own without being compensated. It's typically a two-stop shop. First, the agent identifies the potential producers associated with "buyers" aka studios or independent financing entities. Sometimes, they can also pick an A-list producer without an overall deal for a targeted studio. The producers who respond to the spec will then go into their respective studios for them to acquire the script for development.

HOW A SCRIPT GETS SOLD

Here's a typical scenario: The agent sends the screenplay to producers with first-look deals at Sony, Disney, and Paramount. Three things can happen:

1. All producers PASS on the script. That means no sale.
2. The producer with a deal at Sony says YES to the script while the producers at Disney and Warner Bros. pass. Then the producer submits the script to Sony for them to acquire it to develop as part of their slate. If Sony says yes, then the script is sold. If Sony passes, then it's dead.
3. Producers at Sony, Disney, and Warner Bros. all say YES to the script. And three studios also say YES to acquiring the script for its respective producers. Then you have a "bidding war." This is whenever there is more than one buyer who wants the script.

While this is a traditional trajectory, some scripts may not sell initially but can gain traction or notoriety later on. This can parlay into a sale and eventual production.

DEVELOPMENT AND PRODUCTION EXECUTIVES

The development executives who work for the producer are the ones on the front line reading the screenplays submitted by agents before recommending it to their bosses. The executives are typically the ones who you as a writer will work with on a day-to-day basis in creatively developing the project.

Below is a basic hierarchy breakdown of executives at a production company. Depending on how large the company is, the number of its staff will reflect that. A newbie producer may have a couple of executives working for them versus someone like Jerry Bruckheimer who might have a dozen spread across both film and television divisions.

Principal/Producer
President/Producer
Executive Vice President
Senior Vice President
Vice President
Director of Development
Creative Executive
Story Editor
Assistant
Intern

The development executive's job is reading and identifying potential screenplays and IP's to turn them into movies. Once acquired, they creatively develop the scripts to their highest potential and support the producer in attaching key elements for packaging. Once in production, their duties include helping the producer in overseeing the preproduction, production, and post production. A bigger, prolific company may have separate Vice Presidents of Production who focus on projects that are filming. This ladder is also more or less reflective of the studio hierarchy on the development side. Studio executives there also oversee the deals of producers and respective projects.

GOING WIDE

When a script goes out, it's either "wide" or "targeted." Going wide means to have as many people as possible compete for it. A targeted way is used to reach a few select producers who are most likely to respond. One advantage of going wide is it helps introduce a new writer followed up by general meetings. Even if it doesn't sell, that script can serve as a sample to parlay into opportunities for future collaborations.

ATTACHMENTS

Sometimes, the spec will target a director or movie star before going out to increase its chance of being set up. What can intrigue the stars are true stories or an incredible role that is challenging to them as actors. By simply looking at Oscar nominees and winners for Best Actor and Best Actresses, they are often based on real people or characters who have suffered through hell. If you digested the chapters on the protagonist and created an emotional story in the screenplay, you are one step ahead to draw in the best actor for the role.

WHAT HAPPENS AFTER A SCRIPT IS SOLD?

Once the screenplay is acquired, the producer and development executives work with the writer to shape the script to its best possible draft. Other writers may be hired for rewrites. Once it's satisfactory, the producer will move to attach a director and star with that solid, well developed screenplay. Once the package is set, the producer will give a presentation with a budget and elements to the studio. At that point, the studio can *greenlight* the movie and give the full budget to make the film. OR the studio can *pass* on the project, sending it to turnaround. At that point, the producer can shop the project elsewhere. If another studio picks it up, it pays for the associated development costs.

Every script is like a start-up company with the hope of going public with an IPO (Initial Public Offering) on the stock market exchange. That's the equivalent of a movie greenlight. Most start-ups fail. That's why Silicon Valley investors diversify their portfolios, hoping one project will hit it big. When a script is in development, it's in the red losing money. The costs can add up, from hiring writers and allocating executives' time in developing the material to acquiring rights to intellectual properties such as books, video games, and life stories. Multiple writers are hired onto projects during various phases so the studios can get the best version possible. Through the course of development, it's eating up resources until it gets the wondrous greenlight for production. With the movie potentially costing $100 million, it's understandable. That hefty investment in development directly correlates to the tremendous success of having such a global reach.

WHAT DOES THIS ALL MEAN FOR YOU?

You don't have to master the knowledge of how a movie goes from paper to screen. But a writer should have a basic understanding of the mechanics of the industry in relation to the screenplay. At the end, your job is to craft the script. If the script doesn't sell or get made, you can see how many components are in play. Some things are out of your hands. That's why they say every movie is a miracle.

Chapter 14

THE TEAM
Hollywood Managers and Agents

"We are invested in people's careers . . . not in scripts. There is a reason why I represent the same people today as I did over two decades ago."

—**Robyn Meisinger**, manager and producer, *Anonymous Content*

Before thinking about agents and managers, make sure your screenplays are *ready*. Yes, you should have more than one in case they ask to see another script. Write and rewrite them to the best drafts you possibly can. Representation helps handle the business side as well as supporting creative endeavors while clients focus on the writing. They are essential guides in navigating through the movie making machine that is Hollywood. Key creatives from writers, directors, and actors all the way to editors and cinematographers have representation to help procure employment. When going on a date, isn't it ideal that it's a trustworthy friend who had set you up? That friend saying fantastic things about you is better than you saying fantastic things about yourself.

Do you need a manager to start out? Pretty much. Do you need an agent to work professionally in Hollywood? *Yes*. Do you need a lawyer? It's a good idea to have one.

MANAGERS

Most likely, the first representation you will work with is a literary manager. What do they do? Think of them as real estate developers who are invested in their clients' long term careers. They work with you on outlines, read script drafts, and provide invaluable notes. They are hands-on creatively. Not to say agents won't be hands on. There are definitely some agents who are.

However, most of that duty nowadays belongs to the manager. Divide and conquer. For that service, managers are paid 10% commission. They are a hybrid of the creative and the business. They know story and the market. They can help manage the writer's time. You may have that superb movie idea about robot wars in the underground world of Mars. But they can inform you that there is already a project exactly like that in active development at a studio. Not every project is announced in the trades. Many of them are not. With this valuable partner, you aren't writing in a vacuum which can save you from wasting three months writing a script that will be challenging to set up. But with that said, if you have that one screenplay you absolutely *need* to write before you die, a good manager should support it as well.

Managers are *not licensed* and can produce. If your management company produces your script and sets it up, they waive the commission fee and take the producing fee instead. It's a win for the writer if it gets set up with the manager/producer who has your best interest at heart. Managers can help bring out your creative A-game and help get your movies made.

Below are three companies that I feel are outstanding for writers and am a personal fan of.

ANONYMOUS CONTENT

From one glance of its production credits, you can see the type of stories it supports. As a client, it feels like a place where the artists drive the heart and soul of the company. Its diverse director client roster reflects the inclusive perspectives for a truly global marketplace. While it is one of the power house management companies, it balances production and representation wonderfully. Whatever they are doing is working. Managing not just extraordinary actors, writers, and directors, it produces critically acclaimed Oscar-winning films and prestigious television series.

Film Production: *Spotlight, The Revenant, Eternal Sunshine of the Spotless Mind*

TV Production: *True Detective, 13 Reasons Why, Mr. Robot*

Notable Clients: Alfonso Cuarón (*Roma*), Cary Fukunaga (*Beasts of No Nation*), Emma Stone (*La La Land*)

MOSAIC

This is a veteran, comedy-focused firm that has a rich history of managing Hollywood's A-list comedy stars. One of my former Endeavor agents has since become a literary manager here. She services her writer clients with grace and class, which I'm sure is reflective of the company's management dynamic.

Film Production: *The Other Guys, Bad Teacher, Get Smart*

Notable Clients: Will Farrell (*Daddy's Home*), Judd Apatow (*Knocked Up*), Jay Roach (*Meet the Parents*)

KAPLAN/PERRONE ENTERTAINMENT

Having followed this boutique company's growth from near the beginning, it has always been laser focused on their writer clients. The cofounder is a Northwestern University alum who has generously given his time to share advice with my students in the past. And when he couldn't personally make it as a guest, he referred another fantastic manager from his firm to speak in my class. They both have great character and truly love good writing. The company's clients are regularly featured on the prestigious annual Black List of Hollywood's best unproduced screenplays.

Film Production: *Made of Honor, Knowing*

Notable Clients: Scott Neustadter and Michael Webber (*500 Days of Summer*), Rajiv Joseph (*Draft Day*)

Other reputable management companies include: Industry Entertainment, Management 360, 3 Arts, Grandview, Circle of Confusion, LBI Entertainment, Gotham Group, Good Fear, Artist First, Brillstein Entertainment Partners

AGENTS

Production companies and studios don't accept "unsolicited material" unless it comes from an agent or manager. They do this for two reasons. Number one is to not get sued. Number two is to filter out subpar materials. Agents are licensed and regulated by law. They cannot produce and cannot do a lot of things mandated by the state. Most writers have agents and managers. Even Oscar winners have both. Theoretically, agency-represented screenplays and writers have been vetted and reflect a certain standard. Like real estate agents, they will sell your house when it's ready for the market. They find an angle and identify the best buyers to purchase your home. In this case, they know what studios and production companies are looking for and what writing assignments are open. That gets them a 10% commission. They handle negotiations and deal points. They work behind the scenes to get your scripts read by production companies and studios. Agents are also matchmakers, putting together producers, writers, and directors who share the same taste with collaboration potential.

By the way, even Steven Spielberg has agents. And *he's Steven Spielberg*!

As with the management companies, I am including three agencies below from which I have personal insights.

UNITED TALENT AGENCY (UTA)

It is a major full-service agency, representing top content creators and talent with offices across the globe. Top agents specializing in comedy represent the most sought-after talents. While many clients work on large Hollywood blockbusters, they are very supportive of artists in their unique projects. Although it is large in size, clients still feel the personal attention.

Notable Clients: Joel and Ethan Coen (*No Country for Old Men*), Angelina Jolie (*Unbroken*), Chris Pratt (*Guardians of the Galaxy*)

WILLIAM MORRIS ENDEAVOR (WME)

This company is the direct result of the merger between the 100-plus-year-old William Morris Agency and Endeavor Agency in 2009. It represents top talents across the board, above and below the line. When I used to be an Endeavor client prior to the merger, it was the ideal agency for writers. Although the scope has broadened significantly since then, it is a powerhouse in all areas.

Notable Clients: Gillian Flynn (*Gone Girl*), Dwayne Johnson (*Jumanji*), Charlize Theron (*Atomic Blonde*)

VERVE

One of my former agents at Endeavor cofounded this boutique agency after the formation of William Morris Endeavor. There is a real genuine heart for storytellers, and the partners have built an agency that has earned its well-deserved reputation. It focuses representation on mainly writers and directors across all mediums. Clients won't get lost in the shuffle here.

Notable Clients: Colin Trevorrow (*Jurassic World*), Michael Arndt (*Little Miss Sunshine*), Meg LeFauve (*Inside Out*)
Other top-tier agencies include Creative Artists Agency (CAA), International Creative Management (ICM) Partners, Gersh Agency, Paradigm Agency, Agency for the Performing Arts

LAWYERS

Many writers work with entertainment lawyers. While agencies advise writers on contracts, lawyers will look over them with a fine-tooth comb. Larger agencies have business affairs departments that review long form contracts for clients. For more complicated deals, writers employ their own lawyers. For their service, the standard is 5% commission. Remember, you can't just hire your tax lawyer Aunt Natalie to negotiate your screenplay deal. Entertainment lawyers are experienced in this very specific field. They usually come into play only when there is an offer on the table.

If you have a manager, agent, and a lawyer, you are paying 25% commission! Sounds like a lot. But the way I see it, 25% of zero is . . . zero. Each rep has their own specific role and works on your behalf. The more deals they make happen for you, the more they prosper. If an agent or manager tries to charge you upfront fees, *they are frauds*! Run off as fast and as furiously as you can. And warn all your friends about it. I know wanting to be signed by reps is enticing and signifies validation for all the hard work you've put into your craft. But if they charge upfront money, they aren't legitimate professionals to begin with. You don't want a shady operator with a bad reputation running around as your representation. Ultimately, your agents and managers are *reflections of you*.

WHAT DO I REALLY NEED?

To negotiate and broker a script deal, you will need either an agent or lawyer. They are the only ones permitted by law to do this. Although managers are often matchmakers finding opportunities to work with producers and studios, a manager alone cannot solicit jobs for you legally under typical circumstances. Some writers have a manager and lawyer only. Many also work with just an agent. Very few artists work with just a lawyer. *Bill Murray* is one! No agents, no managers. Just a lawyer. And apparently, Bill has a legendary toll-free number to book him for acting services. I love that.

HOW DO I GET ONE?

That's the catch-22. The norm is you will land a manager first who will work with you to get your script ready. Then they will connect with suitable agents who respond to your work and help attain that representation. Again, you need to build a killer "house" to attract a good agent to sell it for you. Big agencies won't normally sign a client unless they already have credits, sold scripts, or written on assignments. There are exceptions of course. Having a unique skill-set and inclusive perspective can be attractive. Making a splash with a movie at a major film festival or winning a prestigious screen-writing contest/fellowship is also another way to gain interest from representation.

Chapter 15

BREAKING IN
Film Schools and Competitions

*"The important thing is not to stop
questioning. Never lose a holy curiosity."*

—**Albert Einstein**, physicist and
author, *The World As I See It*

*E*very writer has a wildly different path. A lot of professional
writers didn't go to film schools or place in writing awards.
But this way is the closest to somewhat of a tangible strategy. I can
only attest to my own experience and insights, which are the combo
of graduate film school and screenwriting competitions.

FILM SCHOOLS—MFA SCREENWRITING
PROGRAMS

They say the Master of Fine Arts (MFA) is the new Master of Business of Administration (MBA). I believe it! Now does getting an
MFA in screenwriting guarantee you to turn professional? Nope.
But you get the full rigorous training with guidance and deadlines.
Think of it like the National College Athletic Association (NCAA)
for basketball and football. How many college players go pro each
year from top teams like UCLA or USC? One or two? Regardless,

you will gain solid training and exposure from playing full games! And exposure. There's a sense that you have potential from being on a college team. That's the same deal with the MFA. You will be in the creative trenches with fellow writers and inspire each other to do your very best work. Like how the pros draft from top college sports teams, it's the same deal with the MFA. Managers and agents will scour the top film schools for the potential stars.

I had an extraordinary, life changing experience when I went through the UCLA MFA Screenwriting program. I met writers from diverse backgrounds with incredible professions and lives. One was a retired British police officer from Hong Kong. Another was the co-inventor of the Lucida font and a MacArthur Fellow. Talk about rich life experiences! Even professional writers with significant credits return to school to get their MFA. Why? They are always learning. If I never made a dent in screenwriting, I would do the program all over again. *Crazy, right?* I met the most incredible and passionate human beings during my time there. I didn't want to leave! Maybe that explains why I teach. So I can stay in that world of constant connection with unique humans and perspectives.

What about studying screenwriting as an undergraduate? I recommend majoring in something else . . . unless it's at Emerson College. I will go into more details about that below. To be a writer, a degree in other areas will benefit much more in the stories you tell. You can always take screenwriting classes as electives or from non-degree granting courses.

Per my usual curation of the top three, below are institutions that I have personally taught at. Consider them . . . if you are serious about training.

EMERSON COLLEGE—MFA Writing for Film and TV
www.emerson.edu

Full disclosure, I am an Associate Professor at Emerson College. Thus, I'm obviously very biased but can also give firsthand insights. I truly believe it is the best film program for undergraduates. If you walk onto any production set, an Emerson College alum is bound to be in the mix. The simultaneous emphasis for its experienced faculty to strive for teaching excellence while actively working as screenwriters reflects its high standard of professionalism and currency in the business. It is the only college I recommend to study film and TV at the undergraduate level, which is housed under the Visual and Media Arts Department. Recent alums include the co-showrunner of DC's *Legends of Tomorrow*, creators of Netflix's Peabody winner *American Vandal*, and writers/directors of *Swiss Army Man* starring Daniel Radcliffe.

For the graduate program, the emerging MFA Writing for Film and TV program is extraordinary. It is a two-year, innovative low-residency program where the majority of the course work is done online. That means students can live *anywhere*. They don't have to stop their lives and physically relocate to learn the craft. It is an ideal option for writers who work full-time, have families, or other obligations that prevent them from moving to Los Angeles or Boston. Upon completion, students will have a portfolio of short screenplays, feature screenplays, and original TV pilots. As a cohort of twelve students, writers meet in residency for one week during fall semesters at the Boston campus and one week during spring semesters at the Emerson Los Angeles Center. There, the faculty and students kick off in face-to-face classes before going online for rest of the semester. During each of those week-long residencies, a prestigious Semel Chair screenwriter lectures, teaches master workshops, and leads discussions of their work. Past chairs include Golden Globes and Emmy winner Jill Soloway (creator of *Transparent*), Krista Vernoff (showrunner of *Grey's Anatomy*), Graham Moore (Oscar winner of *The Imitation Game*), and Alex Cox (writer and director of *Repo Man*).

Notable Alums: Norman Lear (*All in the Family*), Kevin S. Bright (*Friends*), Max Mutchnick (*Will & Grace*)

UCLA—MFA Screenwriting/Professional Program in Screenwriting

www.tft.ucla.edu

While the UCLA MFA Screenwriting program has evolved significantly since I was a graduate student there, it has a well-known reputation for launching careers of prolific independent and commercial screenwriters. In this two-year program, students can write feature-length screenplays or TV pilots each quarter. The philosophy is to write as many scripts as possible. For electives, there are producing courses taught by top industry executives open to the screenwriters. Those are extremely helpful in gaining knowledge to navigate through the industry. The classes are also great places to connect with emerging MFA producers.

Housed under the same film and television department and modeled after the MFA, the UCLA Professional Program in Screenwriting is an alternative to the MFA. It's a one year-long program where students come out with the completion of two feature-length screenplays. They also offer an online track with real-time workshops that you can do from anywhere in the world! It's a literal video conference with class sizes capped to eight students only. Due to the competitive nature of the MFA program, many students start in the professional program before applying for the MFA. Having taught there for several years, I know firsthand that it's an excellent place to learn the craft from caring teachers with kind support from dedicated administrators. The same faculty members teach in both this program and the graduate program. Upon completion, students receive a certificate instead of a degree. There is an application process with the minimum requirement of a bachelor's degree as well as a writing sample.

Notable Alums: Francis Ford Coppola (*The Godfather*), David Koepp (*Jurassic Park*), Eric Roth (*A Star Is Born*)

NORTHWESTERN UNIVERSITY—MFA Writing for the Screen and Stage

www.northwestern.edu

If you are interested in screenwriting *and* playwriting, this program is for you. Even if playwriting isn't in your wheelhouse, having that foundation as a dramatist is extremely helpful in your craft as a screenwriter. Employing a quarter system, students enter as a cohort of twelve students and write plays, feature screenplays, and television pilots. They work closely with incredible faculty members like Pulitzer finalist playwright Rebecca Gilman (*Spinning Into Butter*). I can't say enough about this fantastic program. The intersection of playwriting and screenwriting are more prevalent than ever. Students come out of the program either as a playwright or screenwriter. Some do both. Chicago is an absolute heaven for theaters with groundbreaking storefront companies producing cutting edge plays as well as the regional staples such as Goodman Theatre and Steppenwolf Theatre. The latter was the home to Pulitzer winner *August: Osage County.* I initially took the opportunity to teach at Northwestern University on a one-year contract while I wrote my personal play *Miki* to mourn the passing of my mother. Not only did that play turn out to be my most creatively satisfying work, I ended up teaching there for three years because of my extraordinary colleagues and students.

Notable Alums: John Logan (*The Aviator*), Greg Berlanti (*Arrow*), Julia Louis-Dreyfus (*Veep*)

Two other institutions I've also had the pleasure of teaching at include the excellent Hollins University's Low Residency MFA Screenwriting program that meets for intensive six weeks during the summers taught by mostly UCLA faculty members. The other is the MFA Writing for the Performing Arts at University of California at Riverside that my former UCLA professor helped build.

Below are more top-notch MFA programs. While I don't have first-hand experiences with these, they have solid reputations and track record. Most of them came into notoriety during the 1970s when young directors broke through and made successful studio movies.

University of Southern California (USC)—George Lucas (*Star Wars*), Ron Howard (*A Beautiful Mind*)

New York University (NYU)—Ang Lee (*Life of Pi*), Martin Scorsese (*The Departed*)

American Film Institute (AFI)—Darren Aronofsky (*Black Swan*), Todd Field (*In the Bedroom*)

Columbia University—Kathryn Bigelow (*The Hurt Locker*), Simon Kinberg (*Sherlock Holmes*)

If you are graduating from college, I would advise to take at least a year or two to do something else. Travel. Teach English in a foreign country. Help out with the family business. Anything. You will be working the rest of your life. Take this opportunity to *experience*. Most writers I know had been doctors, lawyers, flight attendants, song lyricists, magazine editors, start-up founders, Peace Corps volunteers, club bouncers, and literature professors. They have lived. And got something to say.

SCREENWRITING COMPETITIONS

Winning a screenwriting award can potentially help secure representation. But you don't even have to be a winner. Being recognized as a finalist or semi-finalist can lead to signing with a manager and/or agent. It's a way in when you literally don't know anyone. On the same note, by not placing in a competition, it doesn't mean your script isn't good. It's just the nature of competitions that amazing scripts can get lost in the judging shuffle. Be aware of scams out there. Some are out for profit only. Winning a random Bill's Hollywood Screenwriting Award won't mean a thing. The only thing it means will be the extortionate entry fee of $100 that you donated. Below are three reputable ones that the industry pays attention to.

NICHOLL FELLOWSHIP—ACADEMY OF MOTION PICTURES ARTS AND SCIENCES

www.oscars.org/nicholl

This is the industry's top competition that will mean something. Running for over thirty years, it's sponsored by the Academy. Yes, *that* Academy, which awards the Oscars! It doesn't get more legit than that. Winning scripts that have been made into feature films include *Finding Forrester* starring Sean Connery. The semi-finalist round is judged by academy members in deciding which scripts advance to finalists. Five winners are selected from ten finalists and are awarded $35,000 each. They go through a week of meetings with producers, managers, agents, and academy members. The winning scribes are expected to write a new script during that fellowship year. And the writers own the script! Even though I didn't win the fellowship, I was a finalist and met my manager directly as a result of it. You should submit to this with every screenplay you write. Yes, there are over 6,000 submissions but don't let the odds psych you out. Look at it as if you are only going up against one writer. Like playing lottery, you've got to be in it to win it.

Notable Alums: Susannah Grant (*Erin Brockovich*), Ehren Kruger (*Transformers: Age of Extinction*)

WRITING COMPETITION—AUSTIN FILM FESTIVAL

www.austinfilmfestival.com

This is a very thorough competition that is part of the Austin Film Festival which has been running for over twenty-five years. By placing as a second rounder, semi-finalist, or finalist, you'll have access to select panels at the Austin Film Festival Writers Conference that money can't buy! It is truly a one-of-a-kind festival, one that highlights the writers. The unique competition for feature screenplays has different categories by genre. It also has a TV pilot and spec competition in half-hour and one-hour categories as well as other mediums including web series and podcasts. Several of the specific competitions are hosted by Hollywood companies such as American Movie Channel (AMC), Sony Pictures Animation, and Josephson Entertainment. Many judges for the competition and panelists for the conference are composed of respected writers, producers, executives, managers, and agents.

Notable Alums: Pamela Ribon (*Ralph Breaks the Internet, Moana*), Christopher Cantwell (*Halt and Catch Fire*), Amy Aniobi (*Silicon Valley*)

TRACKING B
www.trackingb.com

A relatively newer competition, it works relentlessly to help winners and finalists secure representation. It is created by Tracking B website, a comprehensive database that covers the spec script market. While it's not as prominent as the Nicholls or Austin Film Festival, the competition strategically recruits judges from agencies and management companies to increase exposure of writers directly to representation. Its track record is impressive in securing reps for new writers rather than a direct sale. Many management companies keep an eye on this one.

Notable Alums: Mickey Fisher (*Extant*), John Swetnam (*Step Up: All In*)

CONNECTING

I don't like "networking." But I love "connecting." The difference? Networking seems indiscriminate, netting wide in trying to meet others in quantity versus in quality. Connecting is having genuine relationship with people who you share the same taste with. With that in mind, your peers are the best ones to *connect* with. They don't have to be senior producers or agents. They can be assistants, junior executives, and junior reps. This industry is all about apprenticeships. One of your friends, relatives, or colleagues might know someone at a studio, production company, agency, or management company. Or they may even be one! An assistant who wants to climb the ranks is hungry to find new writers. By nabbing great writers and scripts that are under the radar, the assistants get promoted! They make their bosses look awesome. Those are the ones you want to connect with and rise up together. Particularly in this industry, they can get promoted fast! After two years working as an assistant, they can become a creative executive for another two. Then rise to be minted as director of development. Before you know it, they are a vice president before they turn 30. Prolific producer Michael De Luca (*Social Network*) started as an intern at New Line Cinema when he was in college and got his first job as a data entry clerk. He worked all the way up to be President of New Line at age 27! De Luca was responsible for box office hits like *Dumb and Dumber* and *Austin Powers*. Your peers might get promoted by finding new, undiscovered writers with incredible screenplays. One of those writers might be you!

Chapter 16

COLLABORATION
Working as Partners

*"I'm like a navigator and I try to encourage
our collaboration and find the best way
that will produce fruit. I like fruit."*

—**Jim Jarmusch**, writer and
director, *Broken Flowers*

PRODUCERS

As writers, you will most likely work with producers first in developing your screenplay. They are the ones who went up to bat for you and acquired your script! Or hired you to write an assignment. Producers are the first to see the potential in the screenplay. They work tirelessly on the movie from the very beginning all the way to the very end. They are creatively invested and fiscally responsible for the entire film. It is a tough job! That's why they are the ones who receive the Oscars for Best Picture. They know what they are doing. Once you decide to sell your script, you must have the attitude of trust. Just like when people get married, they shouldn't start thinking betrayal! Just because 50% of marriages end in divorce in California, that doesn't mean yours will. If you enter it with that doubt, it is doomed! *No one* goes into a project with the desire to make a bad movie. It may not turn out to be ideal, but that's never the initial intention.

Producers know story. They've got a track record of past films that connected with the audience. They aren't giving notes to you for the sake of giving notes. Life is too short. They don't get compensated until the movie is greenlit! It's no fun for the producer to just have scripts in development. Like you, they want and need good movies made. They truly want to elevate the material into that beautiful, electrifying screenplay to entice premium directors and movie stars. They see the big picture. They are putting the elements together from the ground up to make it all happen. You are one of those elements. When you were writing that script solo, it was indeed all yours. But as the script moves forward into development with the producer, they have bought into your story. They are now your partner in shaping it.

DIRECTORS

A producer will attach a director who they see will be a fantastic fit for the project. Together, they will work with the writer to further develop the material. At this point, the writer can stay on and be paid to work on rewrites for the director's pass of the script. While you may have originated the screenplay or the adaptation of an existing material, your role now is to service the vision of the movie. The director is the captain of that vision. In this co-parenting scenario, each well-intentioned parent may have different philosophies on how to raise a child. Thorough communication and mutual respect can help make this work smoothly. With the right combination of producer, director, and writer working together as *partners*, a great movie can be born. The best mindset to have in every collaboration is: "How can I help?"

WRITERS

For some writers, they start as a team. Other writers may partner up on a project by project basis. Two heads are better than one, right?

At least two heads that *share the same taste* are better than one. While you may be best pals from high school, when you first decide to write together, put it in writing. Work out the "what ifs." Should a partner decide not to finish the script halfway through, then what? Or if a writer has to take a break due to other pending projects, what happens to the script? What's the timeline? It can literally be a simple, one-pager with bullet points to sign off. It ensures you are both on the same page. With that, you will feel better about that collaboration as well.

Don't assume. Never assume.

Some writing teams will literally write together in the same room. One types while the other talks. That would drive me mental! Every team writes differently. But if you don't know where to start, you can try this method. Work on the protagonist and antagonist together. Break down the three acts into the step outline in the same room. After that, you can go off and write separately. Once the outline is locked, divide up the pages. Elina takes the first ten pages and Alexa writes every other ten pages. That comes out to be about fifty pages each. When the first draft is done, each writer takes a pass of the full script to clean it up. With technology readily available, meet in video conferences to discuss any creative issues that come up. Like in any successful partnership, communication is critical. *Early* communication is everything.

Chapter 17

PROTECTION
Registration and Copyright

"As the world leader in screenplay registration, the WGAW Registry has been the industry standard in the creation of legal evidence for the protection of writers' work since 1927."

—Writers Guild of America West

Once you have written your screenplay in the United States, it enters copyright protection immediately—in theory. But to give yourself a psychological comfort to show your work to others, you can register it for legal protection. Below are two ways of doing it in the digital age.

WRITERS GUILD OF AMERICA WEST REGISTRY

Scripts can be uploaded electronically at the Writers Guild of America registry. It basically puts a time stamp as evidence that the script was created on that date and proves its existence. You can register any written form of material. It costs $20 for non-members and $10 for members. The registration is good for five years. www.wgawregistry.org

UNITED STATES COPYRIGHT OFFICE

The other option is to register it with the U.S. Copyright Office. It's good for the author's lifetime plus seventy years.
www.copyright.gov/registration

Whichever service you decide to go with, there is no need to register multiple rewrite drafts of the same screenplay. The first draft will be sufficient. Certain writing fellowships and script release forms by Hollywood companies will require registration with the Writers Guild of America before you can submit without agency representation.

Chapter 18

RIGHTS OF ARTISTS
Writers Guild of America (WGA)

"When studios employ us to work on screenplays . . .
they're hiring us under very specific circumstances
and conditions because of the union that we have."

—John August, screenwriter, *Aladdin*

The WGA is the union for professional screenwriters. Guild sounds much more artistic than union! But it is literally a labor union. It's the same type of union that autoworkers, teachers, and hospitality staffers belong to. The guild negotiates and enforces minimums with breakdowns of fee structure for practically every imaginable type of writing for film, television, and new media. It also collects and distributes residuals. To become a member, a writer has to accrue enough units through professional employment with companies that are signatories of the guild. Those companies must abide by the rules implemented for the protection of writers. One of the top benefits is providing valuable health insurance and pension for freelance writers that the employers contribute to as part of the compensation.

www.wga.org

SIGNATORY COMPANIES

All major Hollywood studios are signatories to the WGA. That means they have committed to all the terms set forth including guild minimum fees, residuals, pension, and insurance. Once a company signs as a signatory, they can *only* work with WGA members. Once you are a WGA member, you cannot write for any companies that are not signatories to the guild. That's the point of the union. Any company that wishes to work with WGA members can easily contact WGA to go through the process of becoming a signatory.

CREDIT ARBITRATION

While typically a studio film may have hired several writers to do rewrites, they will submit suggested credited writers to the Writers Guild after the production has wrapped. If a writer on the project objects, then it enters arbitration. WGA members on the arbitration committee read through all the drafts without names on them to make the final determination to see which writers receive credit based on the amount of their work that shows up in the final shooting script. In movies, you may see a "story by" credit. That typically doesn't mean someone came up with just the story. It may be that the original screenplay sold by the writer has now differed so drastically from the final product that the writer only receives such credit. For an original screenplay, a writer must contribute more than 50% to receive a "Screenplay by" credit. For a non-original screenplay, the writer has to contribute more than 33%. Many writers who perform rewrite duties may not get credit as a result of contributing below the benchmark. When you see several names in the writing credits, it's not that they all sat down and wrote the screenplay together. Each of the credited writers satisfied the percentage requirement.

LEAVE NO WRITING BEHIND

As creative writers working with production companies, things can get a bit murky during the process of selling a pitch or going up for a writing assignment. This can include adapting a book, video game, magazine article, remake, or true story which the company has acquired the rights to. When pitching, a writer will typically prepare a five- to eight-page pitch document for themselves to present orally during the meeting. With all good intention, executives may ask if the writer can send the document so they can digest it more and present it properly to the higher-ups. Enforced by the Guild, writers cannot send fully written pitches as it constitutes as unpaid writing. The writer has done a giant part of the work in breaking story and characters. Depending on the open assignment, the company generally meets several potential writers, each giving their prepared takes. Especially now as movies are becoming more international, writers are often asked to email their take or pitches to *foreign* companies. It's tempting to do so to get the leg up on securing the job. But it's not in your best interest in the long run and is against guild rules.

IN THE COMPANY OF WRITERS

There are several inclusion and equity committees that a writer can join which foster and promote the interests of diverse writers. Panels and events for general membership not only continue education but also foster an incredible creative community that helps elevate writers in their own work and enhance employment prospects.

Part Four

WHAT A WONDERFUL WORLD
Universal Movies

"The universe is made of stories, not of atoms."
—**Muriel Rukeyser**, poet, *The Speed of Darkness*

Chapter 19

GLOBAL FRANCHISE
Connection and Consistency

"As audiences stay with us and audiences keep telling us, as they certainly did all around the world . . . that they're embracing new ideas and new visions and new places and new ways of telling stories."

—**Kevin Feige**, producer and president, Marvel Studios, *The Avengers*

From my travels, it's always fascinating to see how American restaurant franchises dominate globally over any other type of brands. From McDonalds, KFC, and Subway, to Starbucks, each franchise has a presence in over 100 countries crossing all continents! What non-American culinary establishment comes even close? There is an expectation by the consumers to experience consistency in quality and presentation when eating at those restaurants, no matter what country it is.

Why? They are used to it.

Global audiences are *used to* how American movies should "taste." That taste is how the story is fed to the audience. There is a certain expectation in the narrative structure. They aren't asking what's Act One, Act Two, or Act Three. But they subconsciously anticipate certain moments like the *Big Four* structural points. If they're not there, the frustrated audience will question the narrative. What if you walked into a McDonalds and the Big Mac was missing from the menu? Or it takes thirty minutes to get your meal? The Big Mac is a staple and that's not the speed you expect from a fast food restaurant. It would be frustrating. The same goes for movies. There is a certain build up and momentum the audience has come to expect from films just as they expect a certain menu, food preparation, and promptness from a restaurant franchise. Each movie franchise sequel must maintain the similar style, tone, character dynamics, and even narrative cadence of the original film despite having different writers and directors. It keeps the brand consistent, giving the audience what they expect to continue their emotional investments in the characters and the world.

The *Star Wars*, Marvel, and DC universes are clear examples. In a non-IP example, *Home Alone 2* gives the audience all the satisfying structural narrative recalls from the original. In addition to the set-up of being left behind, the pigeon lady serves a parallel role to the creepy, snow shoveling neighbor in the first film. The consistency and universe-building present within these franchises now resemble the ways television series correlate to their spinoffs.

Chapter 20

EXTRACTING CULTURE
Inclusion of Perspectives

*"Success is the moment we are color-blind . . .
when an actor is cast not because it was written
specifically but because he or she is right for the
part and the actor has such power and visibility
that they can command the lead in any project."*

—Guillermo del Toro, writer and
director, *The Shape of Water*

Slumdog Millionaire. Brokeback Mountain. Get Out. Black Panther. Crazy Rich Asians.

These are incredible films with inclusive characters and story-lines that went on to receive critical acclaim *and* global box office glory. They defied the rules of what can be blockbusters and rocketed beyond expectations. Complaints about inclusion and equity in on-screen representation can go on all day long. Ultimately, what speaks loudest is the box office. Remember, *it is a business.* Those numbers ultimately reflect the huge appetite by a global audience for inclusive stories. Their profitability establishes precedence. When presenting a potential movie project with inclusive characters, comparable successes like these can be used to show its promise. The momentum of movies that reflect our world can inspire writers to create those screenplays with producers advocating them from development into production.

INCLUSION HAS ITS REWARDS

When we itch to tell stories set in a world with inclusive characters, there is huge risk factor that hangs over our heads. It's a challenge for those movies to get made. So why waste time in writing and developing them when the chances of production are near to none? The general consensus is inclusive movies with diverse cast have life in film festivals to garner critical accolades. Sure, diverse actors are cast in studio films. But they usually are linings as supporting roles. After all, the traditional key element of what can make a Hollywood blockbuster is a big movie star. That's the conundrum. There are so few diverse stars. Without opportunities for leading roles to build their stardom, the existence of those stars will never come to be. Since these films are paving the way, writers with flare and fire for inclusive stories should write those screenplays that have been bubbling inside them.

For the longest time, the "parking lot" was full, as a UCLA industry professor once used as an analogy. That is according to signage that attendants put up to steer you away from a crowded lot. But it is never full. Cars are leaving *all the time*. The sign has discouraged those stories and writers.

Until now.

The films below ignored the "lot is full" sign and drove straight in! *All* found empty parking spaces. They took risks, breaking the rules in telling stories with diverse characters at the center. And they were rewarded very handsomely for it.

Crazy Rich Asians (2018) is based on a best-selling novel and was the top grossing romantic comedy in ten years with a global box office cume of $238 million. *And* its cast is all-Asian with no big Hollywood stars.

Black Panther (2018) is the highest-grossing superhero movie *ever* with $1.3 billion box office around the world. *And* its cast is all black with no big Hollywood stars.

Get Out (2017) is an elevated, original horror movie that grossed $253 million globally and won an Oscar for Best Original Screenplay. *And* the protagonist is black with no big Hollywood stars.

Slumdog Millionaire (2008) is a movie based on an Indian novel. It was shot in India with mostly Hindi dialogue and made over $378 million. With nine Oscar nominations, it won Best Picture and Best Adapted Screenplay. *And* its cast is ethnically Indian with no big Hollywood stars.

Brokeback Mountain (2005) is a love story between two cowboys that hit $178 million worldwide and won an Oscar for Best Adapted Screenplay. At the time, Heath Ledger and Jake Gyllenhaal were not marquee stars yet. *And* the main characters are gay.

Between 2017 and 2018, a real momentum has been building. This was not just a one-off inclusive blockbuster movie that could be written off as a fluke. These are back-to-back movies, from *Get Out* to *Black Panther* to *Crazy Rich Asians*! Inclusive stories are proven to work as *great stories* that connect with a wide, commercial audience.

DON'T PREACH

While *Get Out* and *Crazy Rich Asians* belong to two very different genres, neither of the films preached on cultural commentaries. The premise was universal about meeting the parents of significant others and living up to expectations during short visits in the narrative. Both protagonists face psychologically controlling matriarchs who they ultimately overcome by end of the movies. Obviously, each movie narrative went about its own separate *crazy* direction. But they were universally relatable and entertaining at the core. Once the audience buys into their worlds, then the specifics of the cultures are revealed naturally. Coincidentally, both movies scored roughly around $250 million each worldwide.

UNIVERSAL EMOTIONS

Loss. Betrayal. Love. The spectrum of human emotions is the same *regardless* of sexual orientation, ethnicity, gender, culture, disability, and age. This has to be the forefront instead of hammering in about the differences. Let that come across naturally in the world you've built. Once the audience is rooted in the world, they will experience the specific perspectives.

GENRE

Inclusion shouldn't overshadow the genre. If it does, that's what brands it as niche. It advertises the movie to be universally inaccessible. Below are exemplary inclusive films that have proven success critically and commercially.

Get Out is a horror film, not an African-American movie.

Crazy Rich Asians is a romantic comedy, not an Asian-American movie.

Black Panther is a superhero franchise, not an African-American movie.

Brokeback Mountain is a romance, not a gay movie.

Chapter 21

AWAKENING
Crazy Rich Asians—The New Wave

"We don't need magic to transform our world.
We carry all the power we need inside ourselves
already. We have power to imagine better."

—**J.K Rowling**, author, *Harry Potter* series

Talk about crazy.

Released in 2018, *Crazy Rich Asians* alone has made history for both romantic comedies and Asian representation on the big screen. With a worldwide box office of $238 million, it single handedly brought back the romantic comedy genre for Hollywood. On paper, it was a dark horse for sure. An all-Asian cast with no marquee movie stars. Romantic comedy, a genre American audiences no longer cared for. The only element going for it was the bestselling novel by Kevin Kwan on which it was based. While director Jon Chu has helmed studio feature films like *Now You Can See Me 2*, he hadn't done a movie with an all-Asian cast before. A calling to his roots got him on board. And thank goodness for it. The closest comparable to date was *The Joy Luck Club*, which was the last studio release with an all-Asian-American cast . . . twenty-five years before *Crazy Rich Asians*! Also based on a bestselling book, that movie's box office maxed out at $32 million. *Crazy Rich Asians* has ignited Hollywood's appetite for romantic comedies as well as studio films featuring Asian leads. It also sparked major networks and studios to put TV pilots and features with Asian centric narratives into development.

BREAKING RULES

Romantic comedy is dead. An all-Asian cast. No "whitewashing" star swap for the protagonist. This shows how conviction and passion go a long way. Producers Color Force (*Hunger Games*) and Ivanhoe Pictures dismissed those red flags. They trusted their guts and developed the project. Warner Bros. took a risk in greenlighting the picture. Everyone involved defied these rules and gave it all at full heart. They stayed authentic to the vision. Story wins at end of the day.

GOOD MOVIE

This wasn't just a film that rallied the Asian-American community to go watch out of obligation. People went to see it because it was a *good movie*. They resonated with themes of respect and cultural differences weaving through as characters strove for personal aspirations and acceptance. From beginning to end, it was satisfying all around. It didn't rely on being an Asian movie in hopes Asian-American audiences would go and support it. The director and cast worked relentlessly to promote the movie during opening weekend. The Asian-American audiences did come out that crucial weekend. And the *following weekend* as well. This wasn't a movie where the audience felt the obligation to sit through because it was the right thing to do. Rather, it was the audience's desire to see a great story. It's not the Asian-American audience alone that made the movie a blockbuster. Through great word of mouth, the *American* audience made it one.

STARS

On paper, the film doesn't have the built in IP power of a Marvel or DC universe. All-Asian casts in features *not* about martial arts have been generally considered dead on arrival at the box office. The assumption is that the specific identities and experiences of various Asian-American groups such as Vietnamese, Korean, Chinese, Taiwanese, Hmong, Cambodian, and Hong Kong are all so drastically different. That they perhaps wouldn't all come together and support this film like black audiences would for an African-American movie. None of the cast has been a lead in a studio film except for Michelle Yeoh who isn't playing a martial artist, the type of role that defined her fame to a wide global audience. The *story* outshined the need for movie stars. And now, the star wattage is much brighter for the entire ensemble. A consistent and steady stream of movies with Asian leads can create more bankable, inclusive stars. While *Crazy Rich Asians* enhanced currency of its Asian actors, it will take more than one hit movie to continue building star power that is meaningful at both the domestic and international box office.

OPENING MORE STORIES

The hope and expectation can't be put all on *Crazy Rich Asians* to depict every single type of Asian experience. This is the time to keep producing various *genres* with predominantly Asian cast or at least with an Asian-American protagonist in a narrative that's within the American and global context. This means *diversifying* genres. Seeing Asian characters in stories that connect with all audiences. This is where *Get Out* can be a fine example to follow. Explore a genre that's not stereotypical of Asian characters. Yes, do serve up more romantic comedies. It's proven to work! But also do sci-fi thrillers. Romance. Action and adventure. Crime. Historical true stories—*without* kung fu fighting. Hope these genres laced with inclusive narratives fill out the development slates of the studios. Perhaps that hope can turn into long-term reality with a simple conversation and a warm cup of tea to stir our souls with knowledge and courage.

Every movie that gets made is a miracle. A movie that gets made and is reflective of the world we live in is magical.

Chapter 22

LOST IN TRANSLATION
Creating Stories for Mainland China

*"[Storytelling is] always about the characters and
about how those characters express something that
the audience is feeling. So it has to have some
universality to it having to do with relationships."*

—James Cameron, writer and director, *Titanic*

W hen an opportunity came to write and creatively consult for
the Opening Ceremony of the $3.7 billion Shanghai Disney
Parks and Resorts, I was ecstatic. It felt like homecoming. Disney
was adapting its brand and localizing it for the Chinese consumers. The creative and cultural intersection was essential in crafting
the storytelling of the attractions for the Chinese patrons. It wasn't
just plopping down the park from Anaheim over to Shanghai and
making it bigger for more people. That reaffirmed my thinking. A
globally proven narrative structure with a Chinese story can be accessible for Chinese consumers. They are, after all, *used to* that narrative
structure.

CHINA-CALLING FROM MY LATE MOTHER

I was born in Taipei, but my ancestral home "Lao Jia" is in Fujian, China. Having lived in the U.S. since I was eight, I was writing and teaching screenwriting in Los Angeles. China hadn't crossed my mind in terms of my profession. That changed when my mother in Taipei was diagnosed with terminal cancer. Her last dying wish was for me to one day teach screenwriting to Chinese writers and make movies for China. After she passed, I drowned in the dark. Unable to comprehend the loss and despair. Then in serendipity: Taipei National University of the Arts invited me to teach at their newly established MFA Screenwriting Program through the Fulbright Senior Specialist Program. This would be the start of the pilgrimage that would fill the emptiness that had been gaping in the asphalt of my soul.

Back then in 2009, it was one of the first graduate programs of its kind to train professional Chinese screenwriters. Most of the students already had prior produced credits. I was a bargain. I am an American screenwriter who can teach in fluent Mandarin Chinese! It saved a big chunk of translation time since I lectured and workshopped the script pages with students directly in Chinese. It was a four-month course condensed into a three-week intensive where I worked closely with the writers all in our native language.

There, I got the first taste of the fast-tracking modern Chinese film industry. One year later, Feng Xiaogang's *Aftershock* 唐山大地震 about the aftermath of the 1976 Tangshan earthquake was released to $100 million at the box office. There was something bubbling. My heart was pounding with excitement and pride. Can this mean more significant movies made with Chinese stories and culture? While my training was at UCLA graduate film school and my professional experiences were limited to only the American industry, I knew I had to understand *modern China* and its contemporary audience in order to be a part of it. I can't just be a "fly-by" to a film festival here and a film market there. It meant moving to China.

And I did.

Spending the better part of two years living in Beijing and Taipei, I socialized regularly with Chinese locals who are populating the expanding Chinese middle class. They are the core consumers of cinema in China. I met extensively with newly minted senior Chinese executives at studios like Wanda Pictures, Enlight Media, Huayi Brothers, and Bona Film Group. From there, I cofounded Taipei-based The Unison Company 和谐影业 to develop Chinese-language films while retaining English remake rights. Fully licensed and registered, it is expanding the scope to partner on international coproductions of Mandarin-language content as Taiwan grows to become an Asian production hub. As original story writer and producer, I conceived and developed the Chinese-language action thriller *Retroactive* 追击日 about a man stuck in a mysterious time loop with each day repeating itself as he tries to save his estranged wife from a murder. It is set up at Wanda Pictures, owner of Legendary Entertainment and AMC cinema chain. These experiences along with my cultural background fostered these insights on creating authentic stories that can resonate with modern China.

CENSORSHIP

One important element to grasp about the Chinese film industry is that the government categorizes it as a cultural enterprise. What does that mean? Movies reflect the Chinese culture not just domestically but internationally. That's where censorship understandably comes in to protect the brand of the Chinese culture. Every movie produced in China must be approved by the China Film Bureau, which is now part of The Publicity Department of the Central Committee of the Communist Party of China (CCPPD, 中共中央宣传部). The first step is the script. Before a Chinese or coproduction movie can go into production with a proper permit, the screenplay must be submitted by a licensed Chinese company of which the owner must be a Chinese national. Upon completion of production, the film is screened for final censorship approval before a permit is issued for exhibition.

At the screenplay stage, the following are elements to best avoid as it may be challenging to secure approval. These are not hard guidelines, and they are always evolving.

POLICE, MILITARY, AND POLITICS

No modern depiction of corrupt police officers, military personnel, and politicians in mainland China. That means you can't have a Chinese version of *Training Day*, *A Few Good Men*, and *All the President's Men*. In addition to censorship review, depiction of police officers has to be approved by the Public Security Bureau while depiction of military personnel needs to be approved by People's Liberation Army. However, corruption can be depicted in Hong Kong, Taiwan, and Macao. Another exception to this is if the storyline is set prior to 1940s. That is why many Chinese films and TV series are set in historical and fantastical times to dramatize those elements.

SEXUALITY AND VIOLENCE

Since there is no ratings system in China, all movies have to be appropriate for a general audience. Overt sexuality including nudity and depiction of homosexuality as well as realistic and brutal violence can also be the basis for rejection by censorship.

SUPERNATURAL HORROR

No movies about ghosts and hauntings unless there is a twist of it being a dream or a psychological delusion. Ancient fantasies or fables are exceptions as well.

CRIME

While it's okay to have stories about crime as long as the Chinese police officers are portrayed in a positive light, the criminal has to be caught in the end. They cannot get away without punishment. A storyline like *Primal Fear* where the murderer Aaron (Ed Norton) gets away with the crime in the final twist will be challenging to pass censorship. That one is also extra sensitive since it shows a flaw in the court system.

RELIGION AND POLITICS

Churches exist in China, but they are state sanctioned. It adds another layer of censorship review when religion is part of the narrative. Stories about political unrest and protests may also draw additional, intensified review. Anything political or religious that might be fascinating for a western audience may be too sensitive by Chinese standards.

OVERSEAS MILITARY

While two nationalistic films like *Wolf Warrior 2* 战狼 *2* and *Operation Red Sea* 红海行动 both achieved stellar box office hits, they portray the Chinese military might in foreign countries. At the date of this publication, these types of nationalistic military movies are discouraged in order to maintain unison in international relations.

TIME TRAVEL

Time travel storylines are discouraged. It is geared more towards characters going back in time and distorting history. However, its approval chances might be enhanced if it is scientifically grounded, as *Inception* was, instead of a sci-fi fantasy.

WHAT DOES THE CHINESE AUDIENCE WANT?

Movies that stoke topical points of discussion and are relevant *today*. It's still a young industry with an unpredictable market. The Chinese netizens are very opinionated and have an extraordinary presence on discussion boards. 1.4 billion opinions can make or break a movie. The more discussions a movie can provoke, the more eyeballs it will bring to the screen. What's exciting about China is that a small character drama or even a romance movie can make over $300 million at the box office. A great example was *Dying to Survive* 我不是药神 about a working-class man who made available to the public a cheap, generic drug to treat Leukemia. Based on a true story, it tapped into a topical social issue and grossed over $440 million. While Chinese audiences love big action and special effects spectacles, they are equally, if not more, interested in grounded, humanistic stories.

WHITE FISH OUT OF WATER

The common storyline that western writers typically think the Chinese audience would go for is a westerner who goes to China. The perfect fish out of water story, right? Not exactly. The Chinese audience might not care for it especially if the storyline centers on a foreigner who *saves the day* in China. While a western character can connect with the Chinese audience, it's essential to weave in a balanced duality of authentic Chinese perspective.

FLIPPING AN AMERICAN SCRIPT INTO A CHINESE ONE

This seems easy enough. Take that action or romantic screenplay and just plug in Chinese character names. Instead of Chicago, set it in Beijing! It's got the Hollywood structure after all. A Chinese screenplay ready for the masses. Not so fast. Maybe you can use a Hollywood premise and high concept for the set up. However, in terms of scene for scene, it needs thorough localization to ring true for the Chinese audience. Topical and relevant contemporary story-lines have a higher chance to resonate locally.

CHINESE HIT MOVIES

Below are the titles of critically acclaimed, modern Chinese movies as well box office champions. If truly interested in creating content for the soon-to-be biggest box office in the world, these local Chinese movies are worth checking out to get a sense of what's connecting with its modern population.

Box office source from PiaoFang: piaofang.maoyan.com

Chinese yuan converted to U.S. dollars.

CRITICAL DARLINGS

Dying to Survive 我不是药神 (2018)

A small drug store owner becomes the exclusive selling agent of a cheap Indian generic drug against leukemia in China.

Box office: $448 million

Hidden Man 邪不压正 (2018)

A young swordsman in 1930s China returns home to exact revenge for the murder of his family fifteen years later.

Box office: $84 million

Finding Mr. Right 北京遇上西雅图 (2013)

A Beijing mistress pregnant with the child of her rich married boyfriend flies to Seattle in order to deliver the baby. There she meets and falls for a Chinese immigrant man working as her driver.

Box office: $75 million

Dearest 亲爱的 (2014)

Based on a true story, a divorced couple living in the southern Chinese city of Shenzhen deals with the disappearance of their missing son.

Box office: $50 million

BOX OFFICE CHAMPS

The Wandering Earth 流浪地球 (2019)

When the sun is about to engulf Earth, astronauts go on a mission to ensure humanity's survival by sending it out of the solar system using 10,000 propulsive engines.

Box Office: $680 million

Detective Chinatown 2 唐人街探案 2 (2018)

Tang and Qin team up to solve a murder in New York's Chinatown.

Box office: $491 million

Wolf Warrior 2 战狼 2 (2017)

China's deadliest Special Forces operative settles into a quiet life on the sea. When sadistic mercenaries target nearby civilians, he must leave his newfound peace behind and return to his duties as a soldier and protector.

Box office: $870 million

The Mermaid 美人鱼 (2016)

A mermaid is sent to assassinate a real estate developer who threatens the ecosystem of her race, but she ends up falling in love with him instead.

Box office: $528 million

Monster Hunt 捉妖记 (2015)

When a baby monster is born to a human father and monster queen, mortals and creatures set out to capture him.

Box office: $384 million

Lost in Hong Kong 港囧 (2015)

A man hopes to reconnect with his first love on an upcoming vacation. However, his hopes are dashed when he finds himself wrapped up in a murder investigation.

Box office: $254 million

Lost in Thailand 人再囧途之泰囧 (2012)

On a wild road trip, three men find inner peace in the city that never sleeps.

Box office: $183 million

TRANSLATION

If writing the script in English, it is worthwhile to invest in the Chinese translation before sending to the potential Chinese partners. While one may be fluent in Chinese, that doesn't mean they can properly translate a screenplay into Chinese and vice versa. While the companies may invite script submissions in English, the decision makers can most likely only read Chinese with fluency. Even if they can read English, it is their second language. There are select Chinese companies that have appropriate resources or prior experiences in cooperating with U.S. studios to translate scripts properly. But most of the companies don't. And in that case, the scripts will likely be translated by interns or fresh college graduates who studied English for a few years abroad. Worse yet, it may have been translated using the internet program Baidu Translate, the Chinese version of Google Translate. Script translation is an art. Even professional business and legal translation services may not be ideal. There are more and more Chinese graduate students studying film and screenwriting in the U.S. at the major film schools. Hiring them or professional Chinese subtitle translators for the major U.S. studios will enhance high quality translation that accurately reflects the script. Both Americans and Chinese value the written literary word. The screenplay is the creative bridge. Thus, a proper and literate translation can help better assess the creative merit.

Chapter 23

CHINESE FLAVOR
Adapting 5,000 Years of Culture for Global Audiences

"We have rich cultural elements that can be developed into popular movies."

—Jackie Chan, actor, *The Foreigner*

$\mathcal{I}$n high school, I remember wanting badly to see an obscure movie in the mainstream theaters called *The Wedding Banquet* co-written and directed by Ang Lee. It was a Chinese-language movie that was playing at an American Cineplex! It was literally the only chance to see a movie with characters from my motherland speaking in my native language. Seeing someone who looked like me and born in the same country, it gave me the encouragement to pursue this art.

CHINESE MOVIES FOR THE WORLD

I sat in the theater watching the movie with an audience that was mostly non-Asians! There were no stars in *The Wedding Banquet*. The director was completely unknown. A specialty gay themed film, it was made for under $1 million and was shot on location in the expensive New York City. Distributed in the U.S., it grossed almost $24 million worldwide! It made twenty-four times its budget at the box office, making it the most financially profitable movie in 1993 in terms of ratios of returns. Another Chinese-language film made by Ang Lee was *Crouching Tiger, Hidden Dragon* 卧虎藏龙 that made $128 million in the U.S. alone, still holding the record for the highest-grossing foreign-language film next to *Life Is Beautiful* from Italy with U.S. box-office receipt of $57 million. Both won the Oscars for Best Foreign Language Film in their respective years. Both movies unfold in the global narrative structure: "Beginning, middle, and end."

I am a proud American and a proud Chinese. I devour movies from both countries. Chinese and global audiences already consume Hollywood films. Why can't American and global movie patrons crave movies with Chinese DNA and with Chinese soul? *They can.* But they need to be served in a familiar presentation. There are 5,000 years of Chinese culture to offer delicious dishes of potential stories and characters for the big screen to whet the appetite of global audiences. To put it in context, the most spoken language on Planet Earth is Chinese with over 1.2 billion native speakers. That means one out of every six humans speaks Chinese.

To give a backstory to the Chinese cinematic rise, *Aftershock* 唐山大地震 was the first movie to hit the $100 million mark at the Chinese box office in 2010. Stephen Chow's *The Mermaid* 美人鱼 exceeded $500 million in ticket sales, making it the highest-grossing Chinese movie in 2016. That is until 2017 when *Wolf Warrior 2* 战狼 *2* broke the record with an astonishing $870 million! Even with this astronomical box office take, most likely no one else *outside of China* has heard of these movies. Not even those in other Chinese-language territories. To date, there has been no Chinese-made movie that topped the global commercial success like its American counterpart. Yes, there is a short hand to American culture by the global consumers with its food, music, and technology. After all, the infra-structure has been in place for a long time. Not even Japan or other

European countries can compete with America's dominance in its cultural export. That influence goes back to the world's long history of American movie consumption. But with its rising film industry, China has a real shot with its cultural influence if it can globalize its movies. Even for China's local industry, there lacks a certain creative consistency. It has a couple of blockbuster movies domestically a year whereas Hollywood has many *every year*. Until Chinese films subscribe to the global narrative structure for consistency, its domestic films will continue to be sporadic hits or misses with minimal global exposure.

GOOD THINGS TAKE TIME

The average number of years it takes Hollywood to develop a movie into production is roughly three to five years. And that's *if* it goes into production. *Forrest Gump* was in development for over twelve years. Even the U.S. and China coproduction *The Meg* had been in development for over twenty years! But let's not take *that* long. This is a big contrast to how a movie in China can be written, produced, and released all within one year. While Hollywood appears to make movies at a rapid pace with new films released weekly, it's the stable pipeline of several projects that have been in development for many years prior. When the script development and right elements of cast and director come together, then it goes into production. It's not about giving a production team many years to physically make the movie. It's about actively developing the screenplay properly and strategizing the movie's domestic and global reach at the very beginning stage. The box office hit drama *Dying to Survive* 我不是药神 screenplay apparently took two years to write and develop, which has been attributed to its creative and financial success—and that was considered a longer time for development period in Chinese standard. Two years of development is lightning fast for Hollywood!

The extensive development period doesn't just pertain to big-budget movies. Even small budget movies undergo the similar development time as a movie with heavy special effects. It's understandable to desire a quick financial return at the box office, especially as Chinese movies usually have multiple financiers who may demand a shorter time span to recoup investments. That is why a typical production in China works seven days a week and well over twelve hours a day in order to catch up to that turnaround. However, if there is a real desire to make quality films that can take the global box office, a sincere investment of time and finance dedicated in professional development is key in making that a reality.

GLOBAL STRUCTURE

The "Chinese" narrative structures have their merits. Its domestic box office has proven that as well as auteur Chinese filmmakers whose films garner accolades on the international film festival circuit. But if you take a closer look, every narrative structure *differs* from each Chinese filmmaker to the next. When looking at films by prestigious directors such as Jiang Wen (*Hidden Man* 邪不压正), Zhang Yimou (*Hero* 英雄), Feng Xiaogang (*Aftershock* 唐山大地震), Hou Hsiao-Hsien (*The Assassin* 刺客聂隐娘), and Wong Kar-wai (*The Grandmaster* 代宗师), the "narrative structure" of their movies are radical from one another. Each director operates on their own, unique narrative structure. These Chinese masters have their distinctive style and visual signatures. Structure is how the narrative unfolds. And each Chinese director makes their own structure as they either co-write or are the ones who directly hire the writers.

Looking at Hollywood directors, their memorable films all have strikingly very similar structure that's consistent with all major American movies. Their signature stands out by *how* they execute the story, *not by reinventing* the narrative. All their films are consistent in the global structure. Steven Spielberg's *Indiana Jones* has the same narrative structure as his Oscar winner *Schindler's List.* Christopher Nolan's *Inception* and *Interstellar* both have the same structure as all of Steven Spielberg's movies. Yet, the directors' styles are vastly distinct and recognizable.

WHO'S THE CHEF?

The main creative hurdle is the director-driven nature of the Chinese film industry in contrast with the producer-driven Hollywood. In most of the productions in China, producers and the studios service the veteran director. Typically, the director hires the screenwriters who write in accordance to the director's vision and structure. A famous director has the same star power when it comes to movie audiences. People will flock to a Feng Xiaogang and Jiang Wen movie even if there are no stars. The director is often times the lead producer. And the stars are often packaged by the director. It is the director who then shops the project to studios.

In Hollywood, it's the opposite system. The studio owns the library of titles. The studio buys the script. The studio hires the producer to make the movie. The studio hires the director. They are in service of the studio. If a creative difference should occur and the director part ways, the studio will replace them. This is how the American system keeps its pipeline going. In the Chinese system, the established director controls the package and most importantly, the script rights. If a creative difference should arise, the director takes the project with them. As a result, the studio's pipeline is disrupted. Although some Chinese companies are acquiring IPs such as internet novels, comic books, and video games, they still lack the director's development and packaging of actors. Investors back directors on their projects. They don't necessarily need the studios except for distribution. And depending on the project, certain directors' production companies have the capabilities to distribute their own films commercially as well.

CHINA DREAM

Why do audiences of different cultures rather consistently watch American movies instead of their own local productions? Immediately, one can easily shout out the reasons of big "budgets," big "domestic market," and big "stars."

Those are superficial reasons.

The Chinese film industry has the financial capability of high budget movies matching those from Hollywood. It has a growing domestic market that will soon surpass the United States with Chinese movie stars who command salaries higher than Hollywood A-List stars. China has the financial prowess to hire Hollywood talents from above and below the lines. Yet, its domestic film that grossed over $800 million can't reach outside of China. Although the *Wolf Warrior 2* 战狼 *2* production team and the Chinese audience were very satisfied with the result, it didn't have global ambitions. Yes, it's challenging. Yes, China's film industry is still young and unsteady. It's much easier to focus on the domestic market because there is a proven track record. But Hollywood would not be the success it is today in content creation if it did not have global aspirations. A new American player called Netflix now has presence in over 200 countries!

So how can China achieve this?

Professional long-term investment in the foundation of development headed by trained Chinese and American writers and executives with global mindsets can make this a reality. All it takes is patience and doing the hard work with the right artists who truly "get it" creatively and culturally on the global scale. Infuse fresh originality bursting out of young talents of Chinese writers, directors, actors, producers, and executives. Develop stories that are not typical throwbacks of outdated 1980s Hong Kong films and refrain from cramming misappropriation of the Asian and Chinese culture through western perspectives that embody "whitewashing" or "white saviors."

DEVELOPMENT

Story first. Sound clichéd? Heard it tossed around at film markets, panels, and film schools? Everyone can talk about needing a "good story" to make a great movie. No kidding! But what exactly is a good story? And most of all, how do *you* make a good story? Story needs to come *before* movie stars. It needs to come *before* big directors. It needs to come *before* special effects and 3D. While Hollywood knows this all too well, this is something the Chinese industry can work towards getting a stronger grasp of. The Chinese film industry recognizes the need for good story. If a professional development system is in place, there can be high potential for it to become global. Of all the money in Chinese movie budgets, the **SCREENPLAY** is what Chinese financiers and studios spend exponentially the least amount of time and resources on compared to their counterparts in Hollywood. The urgency for investment return hurts the quality of the movie. It's the long haul if China wants to make memorable and iconic movies for the world.

Chinese filmmakers often mix genres and sporadic storylines in their movies, throw in every possible idea and dialogue line they ever had into it. This works with Chinese audiences, but fails to connect with audiences outside of the Middle Kingdom. I mentioned earlier about the Chinese action movie *Wolf Warrior 2* 战狼 *2* that scored over a gigantic $800 million at the box office in China. As a Chinese viewer, it is an entertaining movie. High production value and great action. The Russo Brothers, directors of *Avengers: Infinity War*, were consultants. It had no real distribution outside of China except for some limited releases in the U.S. for the Chinese diaspora, earning $2.7 million. While the movie had no international distribution expectation, it may have had a higher chance if a global narrative structure and character development had been enhanced. As an American audience member, the major misfire in the story development is lack of arc in the protagonist. That seems to be the overall pattern in a good number of Chinese movies where the protagonist is *perfect* from beginning to end without believable stakes. But that is viable for China because it's how the culture consumes local stories. However, in terms of the world audience, they are *used to* heroes having *distinct arcs* so we can emotionally root for them through the movie journey.

Even Oscar-winning screenwriters with billion-dollar combined box office to their names go through years of development with their screenplays. A U.S. studio may invest millions to purchase a screenplay and hire several writers to rework the script in hopes of developing the property to its fullest potential. But if the right elements don't come together, or the budget isn't feasible, or the script isn't right, they won't greenlight the movie. The average ratio of Hollywood scripts purchased to that of movies greenlit for production is ten to one!

FORMAT

Inconsistent script formatting runs rampant throughout various Chinese productions. There is no standard. Feature-length movies will have drastically varying page counts from forty to eighty to a hundred and sixty pages. Thus, the one page equaling one-minute rule does not apply. However, with Final Draft 11 screenwriting software finally supporting Chinese characters, the hope is it will slowly be adopted across the board. While this doesn't seem like a big deal, I see it like computer coding. It's universal across the world, no matter what country it is. When developing that app software for either Android or IOS on a universal platform, it's accessible with everyone communicating on a standard platform.

And that's what a screenplay format is. *A common platform.*

While physical movie production is more or less standardized, the critical issue is actually back at the very basic foundation of the screenplay. Once transnational productions adopt the common platform, it will minimize miscommunication and frustration at the basic script development stage. This will ensure fluid creative collaborations in creating movies together. In China, there is no standard for script format. There is some loose form of it, but it's definitely unfamiliar to the American standard, which has been in existence for almost 100 years.

ADAPTING CHINESE CULTURE

Whenever a non-American film struggles to reach a global audience, it thrusts its localized culture in the forefront instead of threading it through in context of universal humanity. While that emphasis on localization works for the domestic audience, it will disconnect with audiences outside of that culture. In mining authentic Chinese stories that both the audiences in China and the world can connect with, universal characters and story narrative must be in the forefront and then flavored with specific Chinese culture. In Ang Lee's *Crouching Tiger, Hidden Dragon* 卧虎藏龙, it was a Chinese-language film narratively structured in a globally accessible way. To date, it is still the highest-grossing foreign-language movie in the United States with a worldwide box office take of $213 million and earned ten Oscar nominations. Sure, there is action and martial arts. But it certainly wasn't bombarded with typical mindless fight sequences. It centers on the dramatic storytelling more so in the mythical hero's journey versus a spattering of spectacular fight scenes without connective tissue to the narrative. There have been tons of Wu Xia martial arts movies made in the past but none connected to the world like this one. Some critics may point out that it didn't do well in mainland China. But it is also important to note that there were only a couple thousand cinema screens in the year 2000 with much tighter restrictions. If this movie was released today in China's 50,000-plus screens with IMAX 3D treatment, it would have been a humongous box office hit amongst China's sophisticated modern audience.

Although it's not a movie with Chinese culture, Best picture Oscar winner *Schindler's List* is a universal film on a very specific, cultural and historical subject matter. Yes, the movie was made by Hollywood, but it was populated by specific Jewish and German characters. Neither American culture nor characters are depicted. The global narrative structure permeated with universal human compassion and sense of hope connected with the audience, earning over $322 million worldwide along with twelve Oscar nominations in 1993.

Now this doesn't mean adapting Chinese culture requires having to go back in history. Modern stories can resonate as well. While there are no recent comparable films, Ang Lee had done it before over twenty-five years ago with his small, character dramas *Wedding Banquet* 喜宴 and *Eat Drink Man Woman* 饮食男女, both earning nominations for Best Foreign Language Film Oscars as well as sizeable profit at the box office.

By understanding why certain ways of storytelling are compelling to the world, I hope this can kindle inspiration for the creators and financiers of Chinese films to reach for high standard stories and global narrative structure that resonate universally instead of only locally. China has every possible resource at its disposal. Now it's simply a matter of creating those globally structured screenplays with organic Chinese stories . . .

Chapter 24

FUSION
China Coproductions

*"Even mountains and seas cannot distance
people with common aspirations."*

—Chinese proverb

With the explosion of the Chinese movie market, the hill is still steep to climb. Hundreds of Chinese films are made per year with only a handful making it to the theaters. Even fewer garner a significant profit. Tentpole-sized U.S. and China coproductions like *The Great Wall* designed to capture both Chinese and global box office didn't meet expectations. But I am convinced we are closer than ever before, especially with the new generation of Chinese and American filmmakers. At film schools across America, there are a rising number of Chinese students. They are collaborating with American film students, forming fundamental cooperations and friendships that will pave the way for successful coproductions for the global movie industry.

IMPORT QUOTA

China has a foreign film import quota restriction of thirty-four movies a year for profit sharing. The exceptions are given to Hong Kong,

Taiwan, and Macao, which aren't categorized as foreign countries. But most of the imports are given to blockbuster Hollywood titles that help drive the box-office sales. Sometimes exceptions are made near the end of the year, granting additional titles over the thirty-four. But if a movie is a straight buy-out by a Chinese company for a flat fee, there is no limit. While the foreign studio typically pays for all the publicity and marketing, the law mandates a government-owned company to import and distribute the movie for a fee. But foreign companies still need to work with additional Chinese distributors to promote and market the movies. U.S. studios like Warner Bros. have entities in China to facilitate that purpose.

COPRODUCTION

Now you've dived in and developed that winning coproduction that can work both in America *and* China. It even passed censorship after following guidelines laid out in the previous chapter. Roll camera? Not just yet! It still has to be approved by the coproduction bureau. Almost there! It's similar to European coproductions where a certain percentage of financing as well as actors and key creatives such as director, writer, and cinematographer are Chinese nationals. Being ethnically Chinese isn't enough. The individuals must hold a People's Republic of China passport.

Why is there such a drive to do coproductions?

Higher percentage of profit sharing! When a project is approved as an official coproduction where profits are shared, the box office split is almost 50% instead of only around 25% that imported profit-sharing films can take in. Whenever a movie like *Avengers* runs in China, the U.S. studio receives only 25% of the box-office receipts minus certain fees. Various restrictions are imposed on imported films such as blackout periods while optimal release dates are reserved for local movies, a quota of 34 films for profit sharing, and a limited 30-day run. For coproductions, it is treated like a local

Chinese movie without those restrictions that increase the chance for high box office success. Coproductions also receive longer marketing windows without enduring the uncertain import-approval process. Typically, import films are given a one-month notice prior to release dates.

THE CHALLENGES

On the business end for both industries, it makes complete and total sense to find ways to coproduce together. It would be a win-win for both. It is hard work to discover and develop stories that make narrative sense for both audiences. If it was easy, then everyone would be doing it. Here are the two objectives from respective sides:

Hollywood: American films with innate Chinese DNA that resonate with Chinese and global audiences.

China: Chinese films with stories that connect with audiences outside of China.

It is impressive to see the ambitious and visionary attempts over the recent years by the Chinese film industry and Hollywood to collectively capture this unicorn. But something is not working yet. There is cohesion on the financial side. That is a given. It's a no-brainer to join forces with the world's two biggest movie markets. Over the last few years, Chinese media giants have invested in American and European cinema chains, production companies, studio film slates, and even joint-venture animation studios. Hollywood studios have set up local production divisions to produce Chinese-language films in varying degrees of output. American talents and Oscar winners have been hired to star in Chinese productions. Chinese stars have been plugged into American movie franchises in bit parts to entice the Chinese audiences. That model has proven to be ineffective. Some Chinese netizens even find it insulting. Financial incentives can't solve this puzzle in the long run.

The audiences are smart.

They can't be tricked. And they will be vocal on the internet for the entire Chinese population of 1.4 billion people to see.

ALMOST THERE

The fine balance of east and west elements has been achieved before by Ang Lee in his earlier works. His Chinese-language films and its narrative structure are worthwhile to revisit and adapt for today's global model. Some feel there is no need for coproductions. It is much safer to just focus on each other's own domestic and existing international markets. But this opportunity to make our world more connected would be missed if we simply retreat to what we are comfortable with. While there are inherent challenges, both sides are getting closer to cracking it.

WE MAKE MOVIES FOR THE WORLD

As screenwriters, it is crucial to be aware of multiple perspectives. Netflix is making content in its local territories with select ones to potentially be made available in the 200-plus countries that they have presence in. The U.S. studios are working with Chinese partners to create movies that work in China and potentially the rest of the world. It's a long journey. But the modern Chinese film industry is young. It's adapting quickly. The more cultural and creative understanding we have, the more fluently we will be able to construct movies that connect with both countries and rest of the world. There hasn't been a true, organic major coproduction that has earned acclaim and seized both American and Chinese box office. Released in 2016, the first of its kind is *The Great Wall* starring Matt Damon. In 2018, the next significant attempt was *The Meg* about Jason Stratham fighting off a big shark budgeted at $130 million which has made a profitable $143 million in the U.S. and $153 million in China. While the key creatives are comprised of mostly Americans including the lead producers, director, and screenwriters, it shows a promising step towards a cohesive creative collaboration. If current and future Chinese storytellers understand the genetics of global movies, it can establish a common language to craft movies together that can be locally and globally successful, leading to a unified collaboration with American creatives to extract the finest from both sides.

But to do this—

Both industries can work towards adjusting their ego and pride.

It's not easy to have a creative team all be on the same page let alone a creative team made up of two very different cultures. It would be incredible to see the best of Chinese and American creatives come together in narratives that can universally spark the emotions of global citizens. As the next generation of Chinese filmmakers and executives get *used to* the global structure from their U.S. training and movie consumption, it's very promising.

We are almost there.

Chapter 25

HAVE YOU EATEN?
Chinese Cultural and Social Etiquettes

*"We made a lot of friends . . . and just fell in
love with Chinese cinema. We made a bunch of
personal trips back to Beijing to nurture and grow
those relationships in the film business there."*

—**Joe Russo**, director, *Avengers: Endgame*

With mutual investments in each other's film industries as
well as hiring talent from both sides, basic understanding of each other's social and cultural etiquettes is essential. Instead
of saying "Hello," the Chinese often greet with "Have you eaten?"
That alone should inform you culturally how the Chinese differ
from Westerners. Eating is an important part of friendship and family. While Western businesses are conducted primarily in the office,
real Chinese business is done over meals. Depending on the individuals, drinking can be involved. It's a way to feel close to those
who they want to potentially cooperate with. The more you can
meet face to face and be physically available, the more trust will
be established. While film festivals and markets are a great way to
connect with potential partners, fruitful collaborations can only be
sustained with face-to-face contacts afterward. You can't approach

China superficially as a place of quick, easy money. Just as Chinese and global viewers have affinity for American films, sincere love and appreciation for Chinese cinema will yield more potential connection.

COMMUNICATION

Email? Text message? Forget about getting a reply. Unless the Chinese company has an international department, you might have a young executive who just graduated from an American college who will reply to those emails. But if you are serious about doing business with Chinese partners, sign up for one of the world's most powerful apps called WECHAT with over 1 billion active users. 1 billion! It is the ultimate social media and mobile payment app in China. Think Facebook, Facetime, Yelp, Instagram, WhatsApp, Gmail, Twitter, and Apple Pay *all rolled into one.* You can leave voice messages and make calls via video or audio. Users chat in groups, send contracts, power points, scripts, everything and anything over WeChat.

It's instant.

You will get immediate replies faster than texting in America. People check WeChat 24/7. When you set up your account profile, don't just have English. Be sure to include the Chinese name of yourself and your company. The same goes for business cards. Make them bilingual. Upon first meetings, people scan contacts via WeChat. It's no big deal to swap contact info. Westerners are more selective with who they share contacts with. In China, WeChat and business cards are exchanged as easily as a handshake. In many ways, this proves to be more efficient than the guarded approach. Like in all businesses, following up is key. WeChat is your friend for doing just that.

ETIQUETTE

WeChat has in some ways replaced business cards for younger generations. But for most companies, especially traditional ones and government-owned entities, they still primarily use business cards. When handed a card, always accept with both hands and read the name and title carefully. Don't simply shove it into your wallet without looking at it. If a formal meeting takes place in a conference room or at a restaurant, be sure to lay out everyone's cards in front of you instead of tucking it away.

If you have a meal or a drink with a potential collaborator, offer to pay. It's just a small gesture of potential cooperation. Eating and drinking is how Chinese connect. Anthony Bourdain showed us that's how *humans* connect all over the world. Splitting the bill is like splicing that connection.

KNOW CHINESE MOVIES AND STARS

While an American may expect everyone to know Hollywood movie references for comparable successful movies, Americans need to know Chinese movie references as well. Especially, if there is a desire to create narrative content for audiences in both markets. Many Chinese movies are available on Netflix and online. If you live in a major city like Los Angeles, Chicago, Boston, or New York, new Chinese movies are released simultaneously in AMC theaters marketed towards the Chinese population. Watch the movies on the big screen with a Chinese audience. You will gain invaluable insights from what they respond to. When developing projects, filmmakers pitch ideal stars for certain roles. Likewise, get familiar with *Chinese directors and stars*. Find the top grossing Chinese movies in the last few years and see who starred in them. The Chinese movie titles in Chapter 22 are a good place to start. There will be mutual respect from being knowledgeable of players from both industries.

WHAT DOES "YES" REALLY MEAN?

"Yes" means "no," "yes" means "yes," "yes" means "maybe." The Chinese are not as direct as Americans. Chinese tend to always say "yes." They don't want to close a door on a potential opportunity. They want to be courteous. That "yes" might be a "no" as soon as you walk out the door. If initial meetings discussing potential projects feature immediate reactions of "Yes!" and "No problem!" without further questions about details, the chances of the deal materializing are smaller. There are no such things as verbal agreements or oral contracts. You may sign off on a Memorandum of Understanding (MOU) which lays out cursory terms agreed upon. The intention can be genuine, and you may even have a signing ceremony with press snapping photos to signify this milestone cooperation! While this seems solid since it's on paper, it's not legally binding. However, if the potential Chinese partners ask tons of questions, the likelihood of the project cooperation going forward may be much higher.

On the contrary for Americans, a verbal agreement or oral contract are typically solid. A "yes" in the room will signify that the deal will most likely go through. And "no" means, well, "no." If questions of doubt for the project are raised, the prospects will look dim.

LEGAL

The screenplay is an intellectual property. Scripts that are transmitted via that wonderful WeChat app are not secure. Clients at times will send contracts via WeChat. That's like sending contracts through Facebook Messenger! While American writers and producers have agency representation to ensure script confidentiality, the Chinese counterparts may use non-disclosure agreements. To ultimately protect the property, it is in your best interest to register the script for copyright *in China*. That is the only concrete way to legally ensure the protection of that property. While publicly listed movie studios will be less likely to exploit a script without properly compensating the creator, many of the movie companies aren't publicly listed.

CONFIDENCE

The great, late screenwriter William Goldman said, "Nobody knows anything—about China." Okay, I added the last two words to his quote. But it's true! Even if one may be a veteran in Hollywood, don't be a know-it-all . . . especially when it comes to China's very new industry and audience. There are always surprises. The knowledge of the Hollywood system does not apply to China at face value. As Hollywood relies on franchise and tentpole movies to cross $200 million at the domestic box office, small character dramas can do that in China with ease. A Chinese filmmaker and studio may be confident because they have access to the humongous domestic market. An American filmmaker and studio may be confident because of their global reach. Both have the desire to cooperate and cross over with values to add to each other's industries. The more both sides respect and take time to fully understand each other culturally and creatively, there can only be upsides.

CROUCHING TIGER, HIDDEN DRAGON

While the title *Crouching Tiger, Hidden Dragon* is made globally relevant from Ang Lee's cinematic opus based on a beloved Chinese novel, it is a literal Chinese idiom from poet Yu Xin that refers to "talented and extraordinary individuals hidden from view." It's a reminder of not underestimating people. But I see it also as don't underestimate yourself. From inclusive commercial hits *Black Panther* and *Crazy Rich Asians* to China's powerful film market and Netflix's global reach, this pivoting moment encapsulates its essence.

As with all things China, everything is subject to change. The American industry is also evolving, especially with the rise of streaming giants that is redefining movies. The courage to adapt to the fluidity of changes and being open-minded will ensure cohesive collaboration in creating content for the world.

Part Five

THE CRAZY SECRET

"Remembering that you are going to die is the best way I know to avoid the trap of thinking you have something to lose."

—Steve Jobs, cofounder, Apple Inc.

Chapter 26

TO LIVE
Fall Into Place

*"We are very good at preparing to live,
but not very good at living."*

—**Thich Nhat Hanh**, author, *Peace Is Every Step*

C an't believe this is wrapping up. Feels like the bar is shutting down for last call. Alas . . .

It's closing time.

Truly, what a joy it has been writing this book. Thanks for indulging in my spatters of insights. I was a lucky kid to have stumbled into storytelling. But the real treasure trove I discovered was compassion. At end of my classes, I share a little secret that gives life a shine.

CRAZY SECRET

I was 19 years old when I wrote my first feature-length screenplay in ten weeks at a UCLA eight-person screenwriting workshop. I was clueless about what screenwriting was. I didn't even know you could get paid to write scripts. This is pre-internet, after all. I just loved writing in the medium. But what really hooked me was this first day of class. My professor, who would become a lifetime mentor and later encouraged me to pursue my MFA at UCLA, laid out around 100 figurines from all parts of the world. A *community* of little story-tellers standing side by side on that table. Each one so unique with unforgettable expressions sculpted permanently on their faces. I will never forget it. And on the last day of class, he bookended it with this benediction to us. I'm paraphrasing . . .

"It means shit if you win some fancy award. Who cares if you make a boatload of money? What matters the most in this life is:

Be a good person.

And everything will *fall into place.* Family. Love. Profession."

I chuckled out loud. The cheese sounded so Hallmark! I was a kid who hadn't experienced the pain and love of the real world . . . yet. But as life went on with all its heartbreaks and losses, those words stayed with me. In some weird way, everything did *fall into place.*

For real.

Being good doesn't mean volunteering for a day cleaning the beach or donate to the homeless—which are both great things to do.

Being good means helping others *without* expecting anything in return.

Being good means not talking badly about someone.

Being good is how you behave with kindness daily with all humans.

It's however you define what good means. It's a way of life. As long as you work hard and be good, things will happen for you . . . just "not in the way you expect it to." A mentor comforted me with those words when I was first finding my footing.

I hope this has been a useful compass and manual. Update me on your writer's life wherever its sails take you. After all, we are a community of storytellers. Would love to connect: weiko@weikolin.com.

I wish you the very best as you go forward with courage and compassion. In the Chinese culture, we don't say goodbyes. We say, "See you again 再見."

GLOSSARY

8 is the luckiest number in the Chinese culture. The pronunciation of 8 sounds like the word for prosperity. And during Spring Festival, 88 is used to wish others great fortune.

In the spirit of prosperity and fortune of global filmmaking, here are 8 terms every storyteller should know for the Hollywood system and another 8 terms for the Chinese film industry.

HOLLYWOOD TERMS

Elevator Pitch: One to two sentences that describe the story of the potential movie that can be expressed in about 30 seconds to a minute, the length of an elevator ride. It is often used to entice potential financiers, producers, stars, and directors to consider reviewing a screenplay.

Four Quadrant: Type of movie that can capture male and female audiences under the ages of 25 (Quadrants 1 and 2) and those ages of 25 and above (Quadrants 3 and 4) respectively.

High Concept: Describes a commercial feature film of which the movie's premise can be expressed in one simple line.

OWA: Acronym for Open Writing Assignment. When a producer or studio have an existing intellectual property or original idea, they commission a screenwriter to adapt it.

Pitch: Oral presentation of a potential movie used to solicit the commission of a screenplay.

Save the Cat: This is a key moment in the film when the protagonist does something kind and sympathetic which makes the audience care for them.

Spec: It's short for "speculative screenplay." After a script is written without being commissioned, it is then shopped around to potential producers and financiers.

Tentpole: A large budget movie that usually has ancillary tie-ins such as toys and video games supported by heavy promotion on a global scale.

CHINESE TERMS

帅 (**Shuài**): Translation is "handsome." It depicts a fantastic set piece or action sequence.

很牛 (**Hěn niú**): Translation is "very bull." It's a slang used to describe a very cool or awesome character.

敏感 (**Mǐn gǎn**): Adjective that refers to sensitive topic, storyline, or character situation in a screenplay.

审批 (**Shěn pī**): Censorship Approval. This process happens during script stage for the authorization to go into production as well as the finished film applying for theatrical release permit.

接地气 (**Jiēdì qì**): Translation is "connection to earth's essence." This is to see whether the character or story is localized or relateable to the common mainland Chinese audience.

老百姓 (**Lǎo bǎi xìng**): Translation is "hundred old surnames." It is derived from ancient conception that China is made out of "hundred old families." This is often referred in context of the general Chinese audience.

万字纲 (**Wàn zì gāng**): Treatment for a screenplay that is the length of 10,000 Chinese characters.

故事简纲 (**Gù shì jiǎn gāng**): Story synopsis of the screenplay.

ABOUT THE AUTHOR

A writer/producer, Weiko has written projects for the Mark Gordon Company, Ivanhoe Pictures, Walt Disney Parks and Resorts, Don Mischer Productions, The Unison Company (Taiwan), and Wanda Pictures (China). Fluent in Mandarin Chinese, he produced and wrote the original story for the Chinese-language romance film *100 Days*, which released theatrically in Taiwan and premiered in Mainland China as an official selection of the 2014 Golden Rooster and Hundred Flowers Film Festival. In features, Weiko adapted the *New York Times* Notable Book and bestselling memoir *River Town* by Peter Hessler for Fugitive Films and director Lu Chuan (*City of Life and Death*, Disney Nature's *Born in China*). In television, he has written a pilot for Super Deluxe (former digital studio of Turner/WarnerMedia). Recipient of a Samuel Goldwyn Writing Award, Weiko earned his MFA in Screenwriting from UCLA. He was also recognized as a finalist for the Academy of Motion Picture Arts and Sciences Nicholl Fellowship in Screenwriting. A Fulbright Senior Specialist, Weiko has taught at institutions including UCLA, Northwestern University, and Taipei National University of the Arts. He is a tenured Associate Professor at Emerson College.

A current active member of Writers Guild of America West and Dramatists Guild of America, he is represented by Anonymous Content and United Talent Agency.

www.weikolin.com

SAVE THE CAT!®
THE LAST BOOK ON SCREENWRITING YOU'LL EVER NEED!

BLAKE SNYDER

BEST SELLER

He's made millions of dollars selling screenplays to Hollywood and now screenwriter Blake Snyder tells all. "Save the Cat!®" is just one of Snyder's many ironclad rules for making your ideas more marketable and your script more satisfying — and saleable, including:

· The four elements of every winning logline.
· The seven immutable laws of screenplay physics.
· The 10 genres and why they're important to your movie.
· Why your Hero must serve your idea.
· Mastering the Beats.
· Mastering the Board to create the Perfect Beast.
· How to get back on track with ironclad and proven rules for script repair.

This ultimate insider's guide reveals the secrets that none dare admit, told by a show biz veteran who's proven that you can sell your script if you can save the cat.

"Imagine what would happen in a town where more writers approached screenwriting the way Blake suggests? My weekend read would dramatically improve, both in sellable/producible content and in discovering new writers who understand the craft of storytelling and can be hired on assignment for ideas we already have in house."
—From the Foreword by Sheila Hanahan Taylor, Vice President, Development at Zide/Perry Entertainment, whose films include American Pie, Cats and Dogs, Final Destination

"One of the most comprehensive and insightful how-to's out there. Save the Cat!® is a must-read for both the novice and the professional screenwriter."
—Todd Black, Producer, The Pursuit of Happyness, The Weather Man, S.W.A.T, Alex and Emma, Antwone Fisher

"Want to know how to be a successful writer in Hollywood? The answers are here. Blake Snyder has written an insider's book that's informative — and funny, too."
—David Hoberman, Producer, The Shaggy Dog (2005), Raising Helen, Walking Tall, Bringing Down the House, Monk (TV)

BLAKE SNYDER, besides selling million-dollar scripts to both Disney and Spielberg, was one of Hollywood's most successful spec screenwriters. Blake's vision continues on *www.blakesnyder.com*.

$21.95 · 216 PAGES · ORDER NUMBER 34RLS · ISBN: 9781932907001

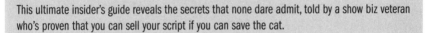

24 HOURS | **1.800.833.5738** | **WWW.MWP.COM**

SAVE THE CAT! GOES TO THE MOVIES

THE SCREENWRITER'S GUIDE TO EVERY STORY EVER TOLD

BLAKE SNYDER

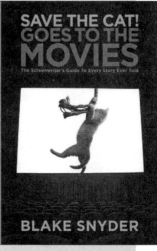

In the long-awaited sequel to his surprise bestseller, *Save the Cat!*, author and screenwriter Blake Snyder returns to form in a fast-paced follow-up that proves why his is the most talked-about approach to screenwriting in years. In the perfect companion piece to his first book, Snyder delivers even more insider's information gleaned from a 20-year track record as "one of Hollywood's most successful spec screenwriters," giving you the clues to write *your* movie.

Designed for screenwriters, novelists, and movie fans, this book gives readers the key breakdowns of the 50 most instructional movies from the past 30 years. From *M*A*S*H* to *Crash*, from *Alien* to *Saw*, from *10* to *Eternal Sunshine of the Spotless Mind*, Snyder reveals how screenwriters who came before you tackled the same challenges you are facing with the film you want to write — or the one you are currently working on.

Writing a "rom-com"? Check out the "Buddy Love" chapter for a "beat for beat" dissection of *When Harry Met Sally...* plus references to 10 other great romantic comedies that will make your story sing.

Want to execute a great mystery? Go to the "Whydunit" section and learn about the "dark turn" that's essential to the heroes of *All the President's Men*, *Blade Runner*, *Fargo* and hip noir *Brick* — and see why ALL good stories, whether a Hollywood blockbuster or a Sundance award winner, follow the same rules of structure outlined in Snyder's breakthrough method.

If you want to sell your script and create a movie that pleases most audiences most of the time, the odds increase if you reference Snyder's checklists and see what makes 50 films tick. After all, both executives and audiences respond to the same elements good writers seek to master. They want to know the type of story they signed on for, and whether it's structured in a way that satisfies everyone. It's what they're looking for. And now, it's what you can deliver.

BLAKE SNYDER, besides selling million-dollar scripts to both Disney and Spielberg, is still "one of Hollywood's most successful spec screenwriters," having made another spec sale in 2006. An in-demand scriptcoach and seminar and workshop leader, Snyder provides information for writers through his website, *www.blakesnyder.com*.

$22.95 · 270 PAGES · ORDER NUMBER 75RLS · ISBN: 1932907351

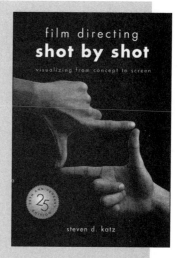

THE MYTH OF MWP

In a dark time, a light bringer came along, leading the curious and the frustrated to clarity and empowerment. It took the well-guarded secrets out of the hands of the few and made them available to all. It spread a spirit of openness and creative freedom, and built a storehouse of knowledge dedicated to the betterment of the arts.

The essence of the Michael Wiese Productions (MWP) is empowering people who have the burning desire to express themselves creatively. We help them realize their dreams by putting the tools in their hands. We demystify the sometimes secretive worlds of screenwriting, directing, acting, producing, film financing, and other media crafts.

By doing so, we hope to bring forth a realization of 'conscious media' which we define as being positively charged, emphasizing hope and affirming positive values like trust, cooperation, self-empowerment, freedom, and love. Grounded in the deep roots of myth, it aims to be healing both for those who make the art and those who encounter it. It hopes to be transformative for people, opening doors to new possibilities and pulling back veils to reveal hidden worlds.

MWP has built a storehouse of knowledge unequaled in the world, for no other publisher has so many titles on the media arts. Please visit www.mwp.com where you will find many free resources and a 25% discount on our books. Sign up and become part of the wider creative community!

Onward and upward,

Michael Wiese
Publisher/Filmmaker

MORE PRAISE FOR *CRAZY SCREENWRITING SECRETS*!

"Serves up many delicious morsels: tips and guidelines regarding both craft and business. Particularly illuminating for any screenwriter considering a venture into global storytelling, specifically for Chinese audiences."—**Iris Yamashita**, writer, Oscar nominee, *Letters from Iwo Jima*

"Demystifies screenwriting in a refreshingly no-nonsense, encouraging way. Weiko has broken down what it takes to craft a winning, commercial screenplay in a clear, intelligent, and inspired way. Somewhere Syd Field is smiling."—**Mike Barker**, cocreator, *American Dad!*

"A truly useful guide drawing on Weiko's vast experience as a working writer and teacher. With one foot in the US and the other in China, he is uniquely situated to give you not only the tools you need to hone your craft as a screenwriter, but also to flourish in the entertainment business. This book should be on any aspiring (or working) writer's bookshelf."—**Susan Hurwitz Arneson**, writer, co-executive producer, *The Tick, Preacher*

"Boils amorphous concepts of screenwriting into digestible, non-intimidating truths."—**Kendall Sherwood**, writer, producer, *The Code, Major Crimes*

"Eloquently lays out a path for aspiring writers to take their work to the next level. You will be driven to write the story that you were born to write."—**Farhan Arshad**, writer, *Man With a Plan*

"Weiko has a vast knowledge of films and filmmaking, enduring experience as a screenwriter, and mastery of his craft."—**Cameron Duncan**, DP, *Longmire, Cobra Kai, Preacher*

"Helps the writer to elevate their work to connect with a universal audience. All screenwriters should read this book."—**Kuo-Kuang Wang** 王國光, writer, Golden Horse Award Nominee *Jump Ashin!* 翻滾吧！阿信

"Weiko is a highly sought-after writer and teacher who understands the intricacies of our ever-evolving industry domestically and internationally. His book is excellent, so it would be wise to learn from him."—**Brian Fagan**, Director of Professional Programs, UCLA School of Theater, Film and Television

"Expands the screenwriting conversation to embrace the global, which is precisely what the film business faces. Using global references, including Hollywood cinema, and a conversational tone that draws in the reader, Weiko illuminates the foundational principles of good storytelling vis-à-vis character development, story, and execution."—**Velina Hasu Houston**, playwright; screenwriter; director, MFA Dramatic Writing, University of Southern California

"A soup-to-nuts tutorial on capturing the international audience that modern-day studios demand. Informative and inspiring, this must-read book is jam-packed with tips and tidbits that resonate."—**Martie Cook**, screenwriter; founding director, Center for Comedic Arts, Emerson College; author, *Write to TV*

"An effective 'recipe' for writing feature screenplays. Beneficial for emerging and professional writers with an eye on global filmmaking."—**Daw-Ming Lee** 李道明, Professor Emeritus & Founding Chair, Department of Filmmaking, Taipei National University of the Arts

"Lin's most important advice is to explore the 'crazy' within you, providing practical guidance on how to mine your *emotional* experience for its story. He explains why American movies appeal worldwide and how Chinese movies differ. Weiko's down-to-earth approach to writing and what to do thereafter, followed by useful tips on how to break into the Chinese market, makes this book your first step to a screenwriting career."—**Paul Chitlik**, Clinical Associate Professor, Screenwriting, Loyola Marymount University, author, *Rewrite*

"Concise, effective . . . virtually everything a screenwriter needs to know to succeed, flourish, and craft professional work in today's movie industry."—**Roy Finch**, Assistant Professor, Chapman University